RECONOCIMIENTOS

Reconocimientos

A MEMOIR OF BECOMING

Rafael Sánchez

EDITED BY ROSALIND C. MORRIS

FORDHAM UNIVERSITY PRESS   NEW YORK 2025

Copyright © 2025 Fordham University Press

All rights reserved. No part of this publication may be reproduced, stored in a retrieval system, or transmitted in any form or by any means—electronic, mechanical, photocopy, recording, or any other—except for brief quotations in printed reviews, without the prior permission of the publisher.

Fordham University Press has no responsibility for the persistence or accuracy of URLs for external or third-party Internet websites referred to in this publication and does not guarantee that any content on such websites is, or will remain, accurate or appropriate.

Fordham University Press also publishes its books in a variety of electronic formats. Some content that appears in print may not be available in electronic books.

Visit us online at www.fordhampress.com.

For EU safety / GPSR concerns: Mare Nostrum Group B.V., Mauritskade 21D, 1091 GC Amsterdam, The Netherlands, gpsr@mare-nostrum.co.uk

Library of Congress Cataloging-in-Publication Data available online at https://catalog.loc.gov.

Printed in the United States of America

27 26 25   5 4 3 2 1

First edition

To Patricia, my love, who saved me from hell

To Carlos Sánchez, my very dear brother

To Osvaldo Vintimilla and our politics of friendship

Contents

Introduction
Rosalind C. Morris 1

A Note on the Text 13

Reconocimientos: A Memoir
of Becoming 17

The Three Squares: Being, Having Been,
Being Another
Luis Pérez-Oramas 111

Afterword
Claudio Lomnitz 117

NOTES 123

THE CURTAINS
By Igor Barreto

> *My silent dream, my unceasing dream,*
> *the invisible wood, bewitched,*
> *where a vague murmur runs*
> *like the marvelous whisper*
> *of the curtains (. . .)*
> — OSIP MANDELSTAM

Life has placed
muslins, very white
on the door lintel.
Now all that remains

is to open the curtains.

Crossing
you will no longer have to
take off
    your clothes.

It's not a matter of nakedness:
The temple lies.
Only what you already have
awaits you.

    You will pass through
an ideal landscape
    that has never . . .
been described.

I suggest
    you release
the narrowness
of this cage

where a bird
shakes a chain
    that holds
a clapper:

that chunk of metal
inside the bell
so its bronze lips
can ring

in worldly places.
There, an "afterlife"
    will be
more festive
and kind.

    So
wrote
the poet Moritake,
    it is:

*a fallen flower
returning
to its branch.*

That would be the meaning:
it's the branch
that sustains
the flowering of a different age.

   Behind
will stay the myrtle bush
with its red
    fruits.

The seeds will come back.

The lilacs will adorn
our nostrils,
our eye sockets,
our ears also.

   Then,
do not doubt
—Go on!
Say it without your tongue

   and think

of the awaited

   word.

TRANSLATED BY ROWENA HILL

Introduction
Rosalind C. Morris

What is the relationship between a writer's life, the historical milieu of that life, and the writer's thought-in-writing? How can one narrate this life in a manner that resists the temptation to render its manifold and sometimes contradictory elements as a linear progression or as the achievement of a conclusive self-knowledge? What genre can support the work of navigating the ellipses, hesitations, and blockages of the inevitably fragmentary and clouded memory that afflicts every subject, without impeding the desire for an account on whose horizon self-knowledge and an understanding of history would nonetheless be rendered visible in their mutually entailing relationships? These are among the core questions informing Rafael Sánchez's daringly intimate and expansively theoretical book, *Reconocimientos: A Memoir of Becoming*.

Originally inspired by a request for an interview from Antonio López Ortega about the relationship between his life and writing as a Venezuelan intellectual engaged with the political histories of both leftist revolutionary aspiration and populist authoritarianism in the country where he came of age, the book that appears here soon became something much more expansive. *Reconocimientos* covers the period of Sánchez's life preceding his arrival at the University of Chicago (where I met him), and then reflects upon it from the late moments of a trajectory that included a doctorate from the University of Amsterdam, recurrent periods of field research in Venezuela, and teaching in the Netherlands, the United States, and Switzerland. From his upbringing in a conservative patriarchal family in which, nonetheless, the stigma of bastardy suffused the intimate interiors of the household, to his jubilant discovery in the plazas of Caracas of freedom and the promise of radical democracy, it interrogates the events and experiences that led him to consider and critique the forces that have, throughout the history of Venezuela and Latin America more generally, repeatedly interrupted the projects of revolutionary transformation, egalitarianism, and social justice.

The book is not a memoir in any classical sense. Nor is it based on a return to diaries, or a private archive of letters and correspondences. It is roughly chronological, but it leaps across the years in some places, and returns to particularly intense scenes from later vantage points. The movement of the text is orchestrated on two levels. On one level, it follows the author's itinerary, from Cuba, where he was born, to Miami, where he was briefly exiled as Castro's revolutionary government came to power; to Francoist Spain and then to Venezuela. These segments of the text are separated only by a blank line that signifies the gap and the sense of departure, but also uncertainty, that afflicted the young Sánchez.

On another level, the narrative's structure is bifurcated. It folds back on itself, both doubling and decentering the account of the individual with an analysis born of ethnographic research and the kind of philosophizing that it grounds and enables. If the first part of the text (it is not really a half) explores the social and political forces that shaped the writer, the latter probes those that liberated him and that remain available in all their abundant potentiality as a force for change and an opening to still-unfathomed futures. The book is perhaps best understood as an extended essay in which the interrogation of self provides a basis for grasping the political tendencies in Latin American and Spanish-speaking history (but also other histories) that have their roots in the psychosocial structures of its various patriarchal discipline-machines, with their phantasms of concentrated power and charismatic monumentalism.

There are certainly accounts of particular childhood episodes and adolescent traumas in this text, along with confessions of anxiety about, and childish exercises of, power. But unlike a diary, which might satisfy itself with the sequential narration of such events and their inner reverberations, Sánchez consistently emphasizes broader social forces, sometimes given form in cinema and literature, and reflects on the ways in which they penetrated into the innermost recesses of a family where he was expected to inherit his privilege as the son of wealthy Cuban urbanites. Thus, in the book's concentrated pages, a mother dreams of *Gone with the Wind*, and inserts herself at the bottom of the stairs, longing not for Rhett Butler but Clark Gable, and a father dances the rumba and picks a handkerchief from the floor with his teeth in a gesture of extravagant gallantry, but is ashamed of his illegitimate birth. Such images are conjured, along with the violent rehearsals of a signature capable of bearing the burden of authority, in a manner that calls to mind Walter Benjamin's memories of his childhood in Berlin.[1] But Benjamin's essays, even when they recognize the contributions of psychoanalysis, do not entail the kind of self-analysis that flows through the pages of *Reconocimientos* and that gives to the work its intense energy, surprising turns, and sometimes heartbreaking scenes of desolation.

Nor is Sánchez's concern with the psychosexual effects of Latin American patriarchy a mere matter of affirming or achieving personal liberation, or indeed recognition—if only by confessing his shame and thereby soliciting the reader's compensatory affirmations. If, in this book, there are faint shadows of Michel Leiris's *Manhood*, with its movement between the intimate experience of masculinity and the tasks of anthropologically informed philosophy, *Reconocimientos* eschews the confident explanatory gestures of the French ethnologist's and museum curator's memoir. Both Sánchez and Leiris omit the narrative of their professional lives.[2] But the reader will find no moment in Sánchez's text like that in Leiris's when he diagnoses the "scapegoat" quality of his personality and locates his revulsion to the police in an early encounter with posters for a play entitled *Children's Prisons*, as though this was evidence of an innate political precocity.[3] Nor will the reader find him recapitulating his obsessions as the almost organically transmitted inheritance of the European aristocracy's persisting affection for classical mythology. To the contrary, Sánchez's text narrates a coming into political consciousness, rather against the odds or at least the invitations of history; he recounts being constantly transformed by experience and indeed of learning, partly through submersion in the crowd, to embrace this very capacity for change. Moreover, in *Reconocimientos*, all the artifacts and edifices of patriarchal European inheritance are tremulous with uncertainty. What Sánchez shows is how fragile, not to mention how debilitating, these illusions of potency are and consequently how brutal is the effort to solidify them.

Terror is a constant thread here: the terror of the child berated by a father as he learns how to read; the terror of the child sent into exile in a strange land (Miami), where not even the kindness of strangers can alleviate the sense of total abandonment; the terror induced by Claretian and Salesian instruction and fascist policing (in Spain); the terror seeded by rumor (some of it planted by the CIA, some of it propagated by local authorities); the terror that courses through the crowd, where every moment of effervescent sociability risks metamorphosing into a monstrous totality. And yet, or rather alongside this terror, there is an urgent, pulsing counterforce, which Sánchez, whose theorizing is still marked by his early anthropological apprenticeship at Chicago and his reading of late structural Marxism, refers to as horizontality. Ultimately, the book is an exploration of, and a paean to the persistent, if often obstructed forces of this horizontality, which Sánchez, recalling the plazas of Venezuela in the 1970s and drawing on his later field research, conceives as a reservoir of egalitarianism and gendered emancipation defined by plurality and mimetic transformability.

The dialectic between recognition and mimetic metamorphosis is inscribed into the book's title. It retains the Spanish term, *Reconocimientos*, meaning recognitions, in the plural, while qualifying its status as a memoir with the implication of transformation: of becoming without end, without telos, and without closure.[4] *Reconocimientos* might also be translated as acknowledgments, but without the sense of grateful tribute. As the note on the text explains, the book was originally written in Spanish, though the English version differs quite significantly from that first iteration. In English, or at least in the context of English-language political theory, the term "recognition" is freighted with Hegelian connotations. Hence, our decision (made after his death, but discussed with him earlier) to use a linguistically hybrid title. We wanted to avoid the suggestion of a "politics of recognition," and thus an association with liberal discourses of rights, or more authoritarian and outright fascist orders of obedience, though both are informed by the logic of mastery and bondage. In the psychosocial domain, as theorized within Lacanian psychoanalysis, which provides a subterranean through-line in this text (not unlike a basso continuo), this logic informs the subject's longing to be recognized by the Other, and by all the substitutes for that Other—above all, the father—that inhabit the quotidian realm and around whom normative family life in Latin America is organized. Sánchez describes his own entanglement by these logics, with the conformist demands that they bear as well as the pleasures they afford. But he also recounts many less hierarchical kinds of *mutual recognition* and finds an alternative to the domination and dependency that normative structures of recognition entail in the plazas of Caracas and in the cultic traditions of popular religion throughout the region. Indeed, it is on this basis that he theorizes "the Mother" as the locus of a kind of recognition that is pluralizing, affectively intensive, and antimonumentalist. Although Sánchez's essay is enclosed, or perhaps better said, embraced by this introduction and appreciative commentaries by Luis Pérez-Oramas and Claudio Lomnitz, the final words of *Reconocimientos*, namely "the future is always arriving," holds the text open in sympathy with that orientation.

Perhaps inevitably, Sánchez's text solicits from its readers a response that is simultaneously personal and politico-theoretical. Certainly, this is the case for me, and I now offer a slightly more intimate reflection on the making of this book, and on my relation to it. The editing of this volume was undertaken in consultation with Rafael during the last months of his life, and in many ways, the process extended the conversations that we began more than thirty years ago. We met sometime between September 1989 and the Spring of 1990. We were students together at the University of Chicago, in the storied Department of Anthropology. I recall that first real meeting when, crowded with dozens of other eager students, each vying for the attention and, yes, recognition of our renowned instructors, we sat around the large table in Jean Comaroff's class on the Anthropology of the Body. Rafael was the oldest among us, if I am not mistaken, but his claim to the role of classroom sage was not a function of his age, or the suavity with which he bore it. He had the élan of a revolutionary from another time, made all the more alluring by the wit and self-deprecation with which he narrated his adventures and misadventures with the Venezuelan Left.

This "other time" of revolution was a territory, a province, and a provenance of both political practice and thought from which we were seeking lessons with which to engage the new structures of global power and neoliberal capitalism ascendant in that era. Although the Berlin Wall fell that autumn, and although the Soviet Union had yet to collapse inward, the epochal transformations that we were facing were already well underway, marked or metonymized by the resistances to them: the Solidarność movement in Poland, the insurrections of ACT-UP in the United States, the struggles against the repression of labor, and soon enough, opposition to the first Gulf War and the resurgence and refiguration of US imperialism around the world. These (and many more) movements and phenomena demanded a new form of radicalism and the creative return to texts that had grown moribund in the stifling atmosphere of the largely patriarchal Marxism that dominated the US academy at the time, even as the exciting provocations of Lacanian psychoanalysis and its feminist reformulations, of deconstruction, postcolonial theory, the Gramsci revival and what, in anthropology, was going by the name of practice theory, seemed to be opening new avenues for that necessary project.

The department of anthropology was heavily influenced at that time by thought about what Marshall Sahlins called "the structure of the conjuncture," but it was also preoccupied with questions of the body, with the "decentering of the subject," with subalternity and resistance.[5] Much of this new theory came from elsewhere and had already enjoyed twenty years of development or dominance in other language contexts, but the US academy, mired in monolingualism, received them belatedly. In this milieu, at once hopeful and anxious, Rafael and I became dear friends, partly because of our shared political commitments, which included suspicion of orthodoxy; partly because of our shared love of reading; and partly because of our shared affections for certain other students, and especially his wife, Patricia Spyer.

Perhaps what enchanted me most about Rafael was his political passion. This phrase is central to the aesthetic and affective intensity that characterized his speech, which was heavily accented with the particular Spanish that is the legacy of his Cuban-Spanish-Venezuelan itinerary. But it is a concept in its own right and one that lies at the core of his (more than) memoir. Passion is perhaps an irreducibly Catholic concept, referring as it does to the ecstatic suffering and ultimate apotheosis in the life of Christ. But it is more than that. Insofar as it names an intensity of emotional experience that has as its definitive characteristic a capacity to overwhelm the subject, it refers to something at once foreign and intimate, which comes from elsewhere but which bears the subject on his or her trajectory with a force that borders on the transcendent and feels utterly natural nonetheless. Something like a drive or *Trieb* in Freud's sense, but unlike Freud's "drive," which refers to primal psychic tendencies, this passion is of the order of the symbolic—and is hence a product of, and is vulnerable to, all the forces of power and hierarchy, violence and repression that sustain the self-reproducing political structures in which all subjects, each in his or her singularity, must come to be, in one or another way, marked and unmarked, sexed and raced, heirs to privilege or marginality.

Political passion is both the medium and the object of Rafael Sánchez's memoir, which is as remarkable for its laceratingly honest self-exposure and self-criticism as for its theoretical rigor and historical knowing. What are its elements? They are, as he himself describes, the scattered images, dreams, narrative vignettes, and sensations that remain from a life that commences in the bosom of racial privilege tainted by bastardy in Cuba, and moves to the ambiguous world of simulacral wealth and subterranean Marxism in Spain, to the Venezuela of oil-soaked nightmares, possession cults, and revolutionary hope stained by Bolivarismo. Yet if Sánchez claims that these fragments resist being transformed into the constitutive pieces of a coherent autobiographical self, as the bildungsroman and the confessional tradition would lead us to expect and desire, they are nonetheless granted their place and their significance in this beautiful text because of his willingness to explore, precisely and without apology, what history in a patriarchal society demands of its male subjects. In other words, Rafael Sánchez has made of his own experience a medium of decipherment for the symbolic order in which he was expected to receive his privilege with gratitude and solidarity, and from which he distanced himself through acts of rigorous analysis and, yes, passionate resistance.

It is not necessary, and it would not be possible, to summarize here the lapidary arguments of the pages that follow. It is nonetheless worth noting that they revisit and deepen some of the arguments that inform Sánchez's earlier book, *Dancing Jacobins*. Yet, in some important way, *Reconocimientos* is a countertext to that first book. Where *Dancing Jacobins* traces the history of monumentalist populism and its relationship to the Venezuelan state, *Reconocimientos* is concerned to apprehend all those forces that escape and overflow the drive for centralizing power. It was these other forces—sometimes voluptuously alluring, sometimes terrifyingly unsettling, always opening onto alterity and multiplicity—that Sánchez discovered when he first arrived in Venezuela as a teenager. He continues to recall them in the pages of this text as the permanent source of radical democracy. They are identified for him not only with a politics of more egalitarian tendencies but with friendship and with freedom. Indeed, these are the three terms of his revolutionary sensibility. They are familiar, of course, but they are also the personally inhabited and, in this sense, actually redeemed principles of equality, friendship (and not only fraternity), and liberty.

Rafael Sánchez attributes this other side, this permanent potential for something more radically democratic than Bolivarismo and Chavismo, to the persistence of what he and many Venezuelans code as a feminine and maternal dimension of the polity, one that is not fully subordinated by the patriarchal structures that nonetheless dominate the nation. In insisting on this feminine puissance, which is variously figured as "The Mother" and María Lionza, and which he experiences unfolding in the plazas of Caracas, he perhaps permits us to understand the political power of mothers in other Latin American nations (from Argentina to Mexico). He also helps us to begin thinking a difference between the communisms of Latin America and those of both the Soviet and Chinese twentieth centuries, in which liberation for women often entailed a splitting off of the maternal function (distinguished from reproductivity) from the political project. Sánchez charges this function with an intense affectivity, an emotional intensity that propels nearly infinite mimesis. In arguing for the force and indeed necessity of such transformations and transformability, he repudiates the destructive forms of repression and the subjective mutilation of male subjects that are often enacted in more rationalist forms of communism, with its ideal men and "new women." But these comparative gestures are speculations that are barely perceptible on the horizon of *Reconocimientos*, which remains primarily concerned with the specific histories and phenomena of the Spanish-speaking and Catholic world, and especially Venezuela—as he encountered it, and as he learned to love it.

In insisting that opposition to the dominant order has historically been as contaminated by patriarchal violence as was and is the ancient regime of the Fathers whose monumentalization and petty self-aggrandizements constitute the legacy of nationalist regimes everywhere, Sánchez offers a rarely compelling text which is as much a gift to the future as it is a recollection of times past. That this memoir was written under the pall of a diagnosis that barred him from any promised land makes of this text something almost miraculous. I know of no other writer who faced terminal illness with such courage nor anyone who managed to sustain such lucidity in its face. Nor is it like anything he had written before, and this fact bears some remark. At some point during his illness, I shared with Rafael the published manuscript of Roland Barthes's last seminar, *The Preparation of the Novel*, and we began to speak about Barthes's "conversion"—this is the phrase that Barthes himself uses, a "literary conversion"[6]—when, following the death of his mother, he felt compelled to write in an entirely new way and, in that process, to rediscover a joy in writing. This new writing would be born of and would endlessly cultivate "a kind of bedazzlement analogous to (no matter if the analogy is naïve) the sudden realization that Proust's narrator experiences at the end of *Time Regained*."[7] Both Rafael and I were moved by this effort on the part of a writer, already so well-known for the veering movements and redirections in his thought and forms of writing, to reinvent his mode of touching others from afar, for that is what writing is.

Barthes goes on to say that "a society can be defined by the rigidity of its fantasmatic code."[8] It is the exploration of this code and that "rigidity," with all the associations of phallic power that this word connotes in the societies in which he was raised, that constitutes the project and the achievement of Rafael Sánchez's text. It embodies the desire to write and to understand what compels and sometimes inhibits this desire to be in conversation with others, even when one is or will be irrevocably absent. This "wanting to write" is, as Barthes notes, "only a matter of someone who has written,"[9] if only, and in the end, his final text, his final communication with others who, now, and only because he has dared to make of his life a text *for them*, can hear what we have needed to learn all along. The reader who agrees to accept this gift will be changed by what he or she encounters in the incandescent pages of this "memoir of becoming."

A Note on the Text

The English-language text presented here is not a literal or direct—if one may use those words—translation of the Spanish. Or rather, it oscillates between a very immediate interlingual translation and something more.

During his illness, and while writing the Spanish version of the text which appears here under the title *Reconocimientos: A Memoir of Becoming*, Rafael and I frequently discussed his memories, arguments, concerns, interests, and questions about writing. Often, he would read me passages aloud, simultaneously translating while reading. These readings became occasions when we renewed our old conversations and deepened them, while also providing the opportunity to speak of contemporary issues. They were exhilarating exchanges, not least because they bespoke an unexpected and long-sought (for Rafael) comfort and fluidity in writing, as well as a sense of intellectual discovery arising from this new relationship to text. When I visited him in Madrid, and then again in Geneva, we continued these reading sessions, which, I think, each of us anticipated with great joy. When it became clear that what had commenced as an interview could in fact become a book-length essay, with a Venezuelan press eager to publish it, we began to imagine it in a comparable—but not identical—English book form. With his illness pressing upon him, and afraid that there would not be time to commission a translator, wait for the text, and then review it, I suggested that Rafael simply reread while recording his text in translation, which I would then transcribe. And thus began the making of the present book.

Rafael Sánchez did indeed record the text. I then transcribed the spontaneously transcribed recordings with the help of transcription and translation software, using the original Spanish manuscript and Rafael's voice messages to assist me when meaning seemed elusive or when exhaustion rendered his speech more halting.. Given the often fantastical errancies of transcription software, it was sometimes necessary to retranscribe and retranslate, indeed to start anew. The resulting translations and new text were then reviewed and corrected by Claudio Lomnitz, who also made editorial suggestions. On this basis, I returned to Rafael, and we discussed questions of both translation and substance, idiom and historical detail or anthropological theorem, political context and philosophical intertexts. Sometimes I urged some syntactical decompression or idiomatic reformulation. Sometimes, upon reflection, Rafael realized that he wanted to say something a little differently, or add explanatory details that the English reader would need to grasp the scene in question. Sometimes, he felt compelled to unfold an argument along a slightly different path. The result is a text that, while mainly parallel to the Spanish "original," has its own specificities and qualities, while still bearing his unmistakable voice and the main contours of the arguments in the parallel Spanish-language text.

A NOTE ON THE TEXT

Endnotes have been provided where Rafael observed their necessity, but I have not added either additional commentary on the text or references to adjacent literatures that some readers may have expected.

Rosalind C. Morris
January 2024

Reconocimientos: A Memoir of Becoming

By Rafael Sánchez

Preserving lucidity with extreme pain is impossible; when the frontiers between the soul and the body become blurred, there is no longer any place from which to exercise lucidity. Pain has to recede sufficiently for the soul to put itself back together as a unit separate enough to explore, judge, and evaluate the vicissitudes of the body. When the pain abates and health returns, the soul forgets the body and embarks on its journey with illusions of eternity. The progress of the foolish soul can then persist in that "bad infinity," as Hegel would say, and go back for a while to its trajectory littered with dreams of omnipotence. There is no escape from this cycle; whatever it does, the foolish soul necessarily forgets the body and takes it for granted, objectivizes it as a vehicle. Written after I was diagnosed with a grave malady, these "memoirs" are composed from a zone of recognition in which the soul hasn't yet detached itself from the body and is still able to make the body speak.

My childhood memories coexist in a sort of blurry contemporaneity. I am not sure that I have what people call an "earliest memory." But I do recall that to which I have returned most insistently throughout the years since—already for more than six decades. I would have been, at the time, five or six years old. I am sitting with my eyes firmly closed, seated in a chair in the middle of the kitchen of the family apartment in Havana. Previously smeared with grease by my father, I hold in my hands a kind of metal funnel or colander while he, standing in front of me, ceremoniously recites, in the style of a Great Magician, a series of formulae or instructions imbued with the promise of some portentous transformation; perhaps some prodigious bird, wings powerfully spread open, will suddenly emerge from the colander I hold between my greasy hands, perhaps some other similarly fabulous conceit.

Instead of such flights of fancy, the only thing poured through the colander by my father was a torrent of ice water that he surely had just brought from the refrigerator. It streamed through the colander from my waist downward, wetting until soaking, like desolation itself, all the inferior regions of my body.[1] I believe I have found the key to many of my more stubborn experiences in the indecipherable mixture of, on one hand magic and the promise of the future, and on the other, humiliation and an inescapable culpability that, for me, is the intimate substance of this memory: from my difficulties with writing to my passionate relationship with Venezuela as the nation that, in good times and bad, both in its overflowing promise and in its unavoidable caesuras, silences, violence, and prohibitions, I recognize as my own.

But this story begins in Cuba. Something that becomes profoundly compromised by the experience of exile, at least for me, is the ability to compose or transpose what is experienced into an autobiographical story, to write or narrate it as a coherent life. And this, even or perhaps especially for someone like me, who did not personally decide to abandon the island, but did so at a very early age as part of a family whose mother and father understood that they could not continue living under the type of regime that was installed in Cuba after January 1, 1959. Exile acts on the past with the force of a hammering, which, with a single blow, shatters or disintegrates everything that was experienced until then. From that point on, any retrospective attempt to endow with coherence and meaning the shattered mirror of that past confronts a series of obstacles.

It is precisely that pulsion, that autobiographical drive, that is irreparably frustrated by the experience of exile, especially when the person is exiled at an age before the notion of a past acquires its body. In such circumstances, one returns from any incursion into the blurred territory beyond the dividing line of exile only with a series of disconnected vignettes: photographs and disjointed postcards from a nonexistent family album. For example, there was the time when I fantasized about directing a horror film on the farm near Havana owned by my maternal grandfather, a very sweet man who had come to Cuba at the beginning of the twentieth century from Galicia (Spain). He had been seeking his fortune, something that he achieved quite early on, when (as if in a film, but in reality) he hit the jackpot in the Cuban lottery, winning monies that he later knew how to invest well. The setting of the film was the fabulous caves, a true wonder of nature, which, in one of those surreal twists that things sometimes take in tropical zones, were actually on my grandfather's estate. I imagined those caves as the domain of a dripping lake-monster. The film's main actors were to be my closest little friends from the La Salle school in Havana. They will remain unnamed, and I have not heard from them since I left Cuba in 1960.

Another postcard: the trips to Tarará beach with my father at the wheel of his green Pontiac, model 1956 or '57, humming and singing *boleros, guarachas,* or *danzones,* while a landscape of palm trees seared by the ferocious sun passed rapidly by the vehicle windows. My father was a fairly successful lawyer and notary public who, at the beginning of his career, worked on a series of relatively high-profile criminal cases that, in their day, had reached the pages of several newspapers in Havana. At the time of this particular postcard or vignette, he was dedicated to resolving the private affairs of a series of clients, and to developing a few initiatives aimed at low-income people.

Of the relationship between him and me, his heir on the basis of primogeniture (although I have an older sister, issues of primogeniture and birthright were, unfortunately, inextricably linked to gender), I recover the scenes in the bathroom of the house, with me barefoot on tiles that I remember as being improbably cold. My father is sitting on the toilet in front of me and urging me to orate in a lawyerly tone the speeches that one day, as his heir, I would have to pronounce in the courts of Havana. I also see myself sitting next to him in the dining room of the apartment, as he instructs me to trace a copy of his signature, time and again, on a blank piece of white paper. His signature would also always be mine, as the double without fissures of the paternal figure. To this day, my signature is a copy of my father's.

I presume that his patriarchal obsession for the monumentalized persistence of his figure had a lot to do with his own illegitimacy and the terrible fragility that must have accompanied it. My father was the bastard son of a rich merchant from Asturias in Spain and an aristocratic Spanish woman, descendant of a Cuban family that, in the last decades of the nineteenth century, had repatriated itself to Spain in flight from the fires of the island's wars of independence and its efforts to sever relations from the "mother country." It occurs to me now that the "Dancing Jacobins" of my later writings have a lot to do with these genealogical scenes, especially if one takes into account the fact that, in addition to his excessive aspirations as a tribune, which were the pretensions of a patriarch manqué, my father was a consummate dancer. At some point, he even won a prize as the best rumba dancer of Havana. My mother often remembered him with his hands clasped behind his back and his shoulders moving rhythmically as he bent down to pick up with his teeth a white handkerchief that had been abandoned on the floor.

I do not need to revisit here the multiform violence underlying the scenes with which a patriarchal order narrates itself in the act of proclaiming its sovereignty. As in Walter Benjamin's essay "The Storyteller," one emerges speechless from such scenes, as from the trenches of World War I, into a world of fragments, debris, fissures, and waste.[2] And it is only with the greatest effort that one manages to narrate anything. Often, one is limited to telling the same story in a different way.

As for my mother, a true "Havana Beauty," the postcard that comes to me from the past shows a Vivien Leigh looking longingly from the bottom of the main staircase of the mansion in *Gone with the Wind* to a handsome Clark Gable, who, in turn, looks back at her from the top of that same staircase. It is impossible to enumerate the times in which I remember my mother returning to this cinematic vignette, or the sense of delight with which she did so. It was plainly evident. Each time, she was, implicitly, the actress and Clark Gable was the good-looking partner who, by virtue of her singular beauty, justly belonged to her. Someone not too good looking and relatively short like my father, could, at most, aspire to being the poor substitute for the North American idol. Someone even minimally alert would not have failed to discern in the insistence with which my mother praised my father's "superior" intelligence, a thinly veiled expression of her intimate dissatisfaction with my father's supposed deficiencies in the realm of looks or appearance — let's call it the aesthetic domain. Because of this, without my being a Clark Gable or anything of the sort, I was from the beginning, and no matter the cost, always destined to occupy the place of the actor in my mother's claustrophobic Hollywood imaginary.

But I will not go on. I simply want to point out here how much, with its claustrophobia and the charge of racism, the world of the film to which my mother returned in her fantasies, and that of Cuban society at the time, were mirror images of each other. After all, the film from which this postcard comes is a true summation of the radical sentimentalization of the racism in the American South in the midst of a civil war that could have been a revolution. Postcards or vignettes like this one correspond to a society in many ways as ossified and hierarchical as Cuban society was on the eve of a revolution that cast it headlong into the disaster that had long since been announced: a society whose failure was born of that very same claustrophobic racism and patriarchal delusion, and that are revealed in my mother's dream images.

In this sense, it is worth remembering that, beyond the merits and flaws of the notion of a perpetually festive Caribbean (indeed the so-called Cuban sensuality and "Caribbean swing" are not just fairy tales, though one would have to add to such stereotypes that of the "sinister Cuban," of which Lorenzo García Vega spoke), the island arrived at its independence from Spain with its hierarchies of class and race practically intact. The slave system was abolished only a few years before independence, in 1886. I still remember people of my childhood bragging of a physiognomic intelligence that would allow them to discern with the greatest precision, and as though it were self-evident, the degrees of racial mixture in one or another individual simply by observing either the color of the inside of their lips, or the relative conformity and proportionality of their ankles, buttocks, cheekbones, and other regions of the body. I think that the Cuban context of the era needs to be taken into consideration in order to understand the intimate stigma that must have always accompanied my father as the illegitimate son that he was, always afraid of being publicly shown up; or to understand the terrible, but also pathetically puerile excesses inherent to his condition as a failed patriarch. Many of my father's decisions would not have been as grave or meaningful had they not been cemented in a society that was as hierarchical or as ossified as Cuba.

Decisions such as that which led my father to marry someone like my mother were, to say the least, ambivalent and full of potential contradictions and likely disappointments. For all her celebrated beauty, my mother came from an immigrant background of wealthy Galicians which, by then, was imbued with the most prudish Catholicism, deep-rooted prejudices, and a rancid conservatism. She could not have been more distant from the considerably more worldly and cosmopolitan milieu from which my father came. If one takes into account my father's liminal condition as someone who belonged to a relatively elevated social stratum, with studies and stays in Europe, but who, at the same time, had always to bear the stigma of illegitimacy, it is not unreasonable to suspect that, beyond amorous attraction, something else must have influenced his decision to marry someone like my mother. Indeed, as a woman of quite rigid convictions and conservative traditions, my mother could not have offered a sharper contrast to the image of his own mother (my grandmother), who, from the reports that have reached me, was quite eccentric and liberal in her manners.

Another of my father's decisions that, I believe, makes more sense in light of the mores of Cuban society at that time was to become a prominent and even famous rumba dancer. In a society in which, at that time and perhaps even today, rumba is a genre circumscribed and limited to (or at least strongly associated with) the country's Black populations, it occurs to me that such a decision must have had something to do with my father's status as someone who was at the same time central and marginal with respect to the prevailing social hierarchies. It seems to me that such liminality might have conferred a certain license to transgress, a license that, paradoxically, would have projected him from the sublunary world of Havana rumba to the heights from which, at least provisionally, the stigma of his origins could recede from visibility. And all this while he tacitly boasted that he was at least as good at dancing rumba, if not better, than were Black people. Those, I think, must have been some of the secret springs animating my father's decisions and behavior. Beyond what people have actually done with their lives, in a society like that of Cuba, decisions like my father's acquired a greater meaning and acquired a more portentous significance. In a society where the most ferocious prejudices are often nothing more than an instrument for the protection of the most prohibitively conservative and exclusionary institutions—such as the family, presumed genealogical conceits, and alleged racial or class purities—painful attacks on such institutions always came from the "outside." And my father's seemingly strange decisions were part of a fraught game of belonging. Both in terms of their transgression of and subjection to the prevailing norms, these decisions were, I believe, already stamped by their time and place. Here, the contrast between societies such as Cuba and Venezuela is highly illuminating.

Of course, my milieu extended beyond the triangle with my parents in which I was positioned as heir. My schooling until the second grade took place at the Lafayette School in Havana, a bilingual institution where half of the instruction was in Spanish and the other half was in English. From that experience, I remember my kindergarten teacher urging us to take cover under the classroom desks to avoid the gunshots that could be heard outside and that were associated with the revolutionary activities against Batista. (Or was it simply a simulacrum, an exercise of simulation? I don't know. Memory incessantly rewrites itself.)

I also remember the occasion when, seeking to impute to us a kind of mutual infatuation, the children of the room, from their respective seats and surely at the teacher's behest, chanted and sang the notes of a wedding hymn around me and a girl in the class, both of us standing as they did so. Unmasking us in front of everyone as a pair of "dependent infants," pathetically in need of the care, attentions, and affections of others but somehow separate from them, that micro-ritual of collective humiliation surely contained some truth. As the best students of the class, we seemed destined for each other in the extremely boring universe that has always been in store for model students, those who in Venezuela are called "cocks" or "roosters" and in Spain, "nerds" [*empollones*]. Be that as it may, judging from the profound embarrassment and the intense heat that rose to my cheeks (and that returns to me even now) as my companions reeled off the notes of the nuptial hymn, the ritual of unmasking clearly hit the target—at least as far as I was concerned. As someone who had been caught red-handed, discovered in public to have perpetrated some improper bodily act, my sense of humiliation could not have been more complete.

Finally, of my passage through Lafayette School, I remember the occasion on which a little classmate sitting at my side in the last row of the first class, called my attention from his desk to show me the great skill and dexterity with which he could stretch his testicles, implausibly unfolding them to the side like the wings of a pallid bat. So far, so good. But problems emerged when, obeying my mother's harsh instructions ("It is enough for someone to simply touch your buttocks or any other part of your body for you to immediately report what happened"), I told her about my little classmate's feats in the order of Chiroptera (bats). From then on, all was a succession of catastrophes: from the meeting in the school office between my parents and those of the other child, where both he and I were present, to the decision, made in a fit of indignation on my parents' part, to transfer me to the LaSalle School, also in Havana, where I attended third and fourth grades. To this day, I remember the episode with a sense of shame, as if washed by one of the waves of moral panic that reached the island from the United States, propelled, I imagine, by the media, especially television, in which Cuba was a pioneer in Latin America. Likewise, the decision to have me circumcised at no less than seven years old, because, according to the wisdom of the time, "that was what was most hygienic," was part of that same crusading spirit.

From my time at LaSalle, I remember the wide central courtyard with morning sunlight and the hustle and bustle of schoolchildren in their uniforms, suddenly crowding around two who were showering each other with *piñazos*, as they called "punches" in Cuba, while the others cheered them on. In my memory, the blood flows red. Also, the spacious classrooms with high ceilings, full of mahogany-colored desks. On one of side of the room, we form a long column as the teacher, sitting behind a desk at the front of the room, calls us by our names according to the position that each of us had achieved in recognition of our academic merits.

Or the day when, once again instigated by my mother, I made a colorful drawing in art class on the topic of the agrarian reform then in progress, with cows, trees, pigs, and other such specimens represented upside down, as in the "upside down world" of carnivalesque rituals and other popular insurrections so studied by historians. Or when, surely as part of the preparation for my first communion, I confessed on my knees to the priest how much I "hated" Fidel Castro. As one would expect, such a "confession" did not emerge from any interiority of my own. Far from it. By announcing this mortal sin, hatred, to the priest I was merely parroting what, just a few days earlier, I had offered my mother when, in preparation for this confession, we were reviewing together a list of my possible sins. "Yes, Mother. Of course, mea culpa, I hate him." What else could I do but confirm to her that in addition to all the other sins, I, her son, was also truly guilty of the capital sin of hating, to the very end, the new Cuban leader? Made with great gravity, as she looked me squarely in the eyes, my mother posed her question—"isn't it true that you . . . etc.?" I did not admit any equivocation; my sinful crime of lèse majesté was prescribed in advance by maternal demand. By then, with the revolutionaries barely ascendant, she was already a melancholic Vivian Leigh, contemplating her world being devoured by the flames fanned by the plebians. As for me, my only interest at the time, as the island was immersed in conflagration, was with the bullets that I requested with the spirit of a compulsive collector from the bearded men (the troops of Fidel) scattered throughout

Havana. I asked for these along with the little stamps bearing images of the revolution, which I exchanged with other schoolboys. I still remember one dedicated to *Granma*—the yacht that brought Fidel and his companions, eighty-two of them, to disembark in Cuba in November 1956.

Curiously enough, none of the memories I have of my school years include any of my two closest friends from LaSalle, whom I have already mentioned. No matter how much I try, I can't find them in the playground during recess, or in the classrooms, or anywhere else in the school of my memory. In the few recollections that I still retain, I am always alone at the school, always observing at a distance, like the aperture of a camera, the scenes unfolding around me in the mode of a spectacle. It does not take much intellectual effort to understand the reasons for this absence, however. A true Bermuda Triangle: if there is something that for many years was irreparably ruined by the relationship with my parents, it was the capacity to assert myself in public without the fear that the world would come crashing down, literally, on top of me.

When one's father is, like everyone else's, a failed patriarch, with the difference, however, that perhaps his seams were more visible, and when one's mother is a narcissist, as mine was, the most basic principle of survival requires that one systematically play dumb, withdrawing into oneself without ever being fully present. The owner of a tavern in a village in Galicia where my grandparents had a house used the phrase, "That boy lives in the clouds all the time." Apparently, he was referring to me when I was ten years old and after we had already left Cuba, suggesting that the boy in question, namely me, had gone a little mad, or was, as they say, simply "gone." When the alternative is being frozen in terror, thanks to a scream or a slap from your father, or being paraded in front of your mother's friends in absurdly short shorts like a trophy, so that they could indulge themselves as they pleased with the supposed sculptural beauty of your legs, to get lost in the clouds would seem to be the most appropriate response. My mother, by the way, regularly enlisted me for the role of Ring Boy for the weddings of her acquaintances. I still have photographs of myself when I was five or six years old, dressed in tails, looking at the camera with great composure.

In words that have been criticized for being antifeminist, but that nonetheless resonate with my experience, Jacques Lacan somewhere speaks of the phallus as the stake that the father puts in the crocodile mother's mouth, in order to prevent her from swallowing her progeny.[3] Not only did my father never do that—for years, my mother's enlarged mouth, with lips painted obscenely red, persecuted me as a hallucination. My father spent his life aspiring to be symbolically included in her marriage bed, while having to deal on a day-to-day basis and despite himself with her firstborn son, in a duel where love was fatally seasoned with rivalry, abuse, fear, and humiliation. That there was love is undoubted; that there was such fatal rivalry is equally certain.

Often presided over and tacitly instigated by a gallery of grim "heroes of the fatherland," I think that the authoritarianism reigning in the failed democracies of "Our America" (that's the title of the wonderful memoir by Claudio Lomnitz[4]) is nourished precisely by the mimetically contagious circulation, throughout the social body, of fear, as the turbidly enveloping atmosphere that penetrates practically everything. It is a stream or torrent to which, far from being foreign, our monumentalized heroes contribute intensely as accomplices, continuously imbuing the flow of terror with their "founding violence." Thus, in a splendid poem by Adalber Salas Hernández entitled "Carta de Jamaica," which virtually rewrites Bolívar's famous "Letter from Jamaica," this history of violence and brutality becomes one with Bolívar, becoming like the sinews and tendons of his heroic body.[5] In the poem, the voice of that violence speaks through his mouth and is neither foreign nor from afar. A sinister to and fro of insults, blows, obscene instigations, forms of discipline, modalities of punishment, and intimidation destabilizes any supposedly canonical distinction between exclusively "public" spheres, and exclusively private domains. It is precisely in that space of resonances and reverberations that "the great Fear" coagulates as the medium through which everything inevitably and fatefully passes, from the most anodyne glances, gestures, and movements, to the most supposedly transcendent events. When such a mess is confronted by one of those supposedly emancipatory revolutions that, like a plague, cyclically afflicts our countries, then the response, often enough, is: "turn off the lights and let's get out of here." This is the smoking ruin that more than seven million Venezuelan migrants have left behind in recent years.

Beyond forms of everyday reality south of the Rio Grande—where, amid the ruins, and in tension with other forces and pulsions, there often beats a contagious affectivity and genuine democratic drive—public life often adopts a Manichean aspect in political spaces that are forbiddingly divided into two categories of "citizen." On the one hand are those who, either blindly or deliberately, often in a tone of sinister joking, mimetically reproduce the abuse, the subjection, the annihilation even, of others who, on another plane or in another domain, are executed by mafias or less organized syndicates. In a series of dazzling master classes for Mexico's Colegio Nacional focused on that country, Claudio Lomnitz has shed light on precisely the type of states that have recently emerged in many parts of Latin America, where governability emerges from the tensions, alliances, and hybridizations between "official" and "unofficial" sectors, whose common sign is that neither has the capacity to exercise the monopoly of violence. On the other hand are those other citizens for whom action is an abyss, the terrifying gap in front of which people either pass, crouching in fear, or from which they simply recoil, like a legion of vacant eyes hermetically retreating. As one might expect in this dizzying game of mirrors, the boundaries between the "public" and the "private" continually blur to the point that it is difficult, if not impossible, to say who emulates whom, whether it is the paterfamilias who imitates the ruler, judge, or police agent, or if it is simply the other way around.

Unfortunately, in these democracies very little of action and experience is understood as an eminently literary exercise, and democracy is rarely considered in need of literature, an ideal that Derrida implicitly invoked when he said, "No literature without democracy, no democracy without literature."[6] True democracy would, for Derrida, come into being not only through action, at least not action as a punctual or eventful act, but rather would be imbued with vulnerability; it would be action as a proliferation, combination and recombination of signs in the interest of the greatest possible "freedom" and "equality." In other words, action as an essentially democratic exercise involves a game of presences and absences beyond all "authorial" control, which, in its unappropriated singularity, remains open to the future or what is to come, free of the fear that, if only by chance, the party ends with a brutal melee.

"You say that you seek protections in the Constitution!," a joke goes. "Come here then, and I will beat you with the Constitution." That joke circulated in Venezuela until a few years ago. The second constitution alluded to in the joke was the police baton of a uniformed officer. Fortunately, during my years at LaSalle, I was big enough and sufficiently strong enough to defend myself against anyone who tried to hit me, not with a punch capable of drawing blood—that action was the special prerogative of other "heroes" of the school—but with a timely chokehold, by which I subdued the aggressor while on the floor. It's not surprising that in such circumstances I have erased my most beloved friends from places of danger, like school, to shelter them in regions of refuge where, for example, it was possible to fantasize about a cinematic monster emerging from some stagnant lagoon under a vault of chalky white stalactites.

Regarding the rest of my immediate family, besides me, there was my sister, about three years older than me (to whom I have already made reference), and a brother, "The Surprise," about ten and a half years younger than me. The nickname comes from the fact of his having arrived unexpectedly in the midst of the revolution. According to my calculations, my brother would have been about ten months old when my mother had to carry him into exile through the Havana airport. She would have been about forty years old at the time. Of my two siblings, I will say only this: that all three of us bear the marks of having been born into a family like ours, each one in their own way, of course, depending on the place that, for reasons of age and gender, was assigned in the family environment.

Under the same family roof, there also lived three domestic employees, "the maids" as they were called at the time: a cook and two "Tatas" or caregivers, one for my sister, called Dominga, and my tata, Agustina. As happens in families like mine where, beyond weekends and other special occasions, let's call them "stellar," the parents were absent much of the time, a good part of the maternal care was performed by the Tatas. This was especially the case in homes like mine, where mothers sleep until the late hours of the morning and the afternoons are, for example, spent playing canasta with friends in social clubs like the Biltmore in Havana, where my mother went almost every afternoon. As for my father, during the week we generally saw him at lunchtime.

But, of course, I exaggerate. I remember my mother, during long hours sitting by my side, teaching me to read and write, or inventing fabulous stories that I listened to, fascinated. In them, my father and one of his best friends appeared as a pair of big noses who were also dwarf jewelers diligently extracting and meticulously evaluating with their respective magnifying glasses the value of diamonds during their runs through the labyrinthine underground corridors of some mine in South Africa (the imagery is now disturbing to me).

I remember, too, the two-months-long tour of the East Coast from Miami to New York with my father at the wheel. I was about six years old. Both for me and for my sister the highlights of the journey were the roadside motels with swimming pools, to which we arrived at the end of each afternoon after a long day of driving. Even if it's only briefly, I would like to refer to my Tata, Agustina, whom I adored, and who frequently took me with her on the bus or *Guagua*, as it was called in Cuba, to visit her family in her hometown of Güines. From her trips to this little town also came the string of animals, from chicks to ducks, that, to my delight, periodically made their appearance in our apartment in Havana, only to disappear shortly afterward in a certain shroud of mystery. Of these, I especially remember the wonderfully fat, black and white rabbit that appears in a photo that I still have, sleeping in the bed next to me, and that, after a while, followed the same pattern of disappearances, but only after having eaten the curtains—and a good portion of the shoes in the house. To this day I wonder if his destiny wasn't to end in one of the stews at some family lunch.

Of the rest, beyond my immediate family, there was the

house of my Galician grandparents in the El Vedado neighborhood, where we frequently spent Christmas with them and sometimes with my mother's brother and Aunt Haydee, his wife, plus my two first cousins, all gathered around a leafy Christmas tree that I remember as being enormous and generously illuminated. As the most liberal and left-wing member of the family, Uncle Adolfo was for many years a sort of model for me, the only promisingly redeeming figure in such a conservative family. My uncle was also the owner of a bookstore that had the beautiful name of El Gato de Papel (the paper cat), and was located right next to El Gato Negro (the black cat), which is what my grandfather's lottery business was called. The iconic objects of those Christmas gatherings: the boxed gifts piled at the base of the tree and wrapped in multicolored paper; the bottles of white and red Marqués de Riscal wine purchased by my grandfather and carefully lined up on a table in the dining room or living room. This was my family universe, including its difficult love, at least as I can summon its images from the eve of our leaving Cuba for exile, in the direction of the "North."

I left Cuba in September 1960, a few months before the rest of the family. It all had to do with the rumors propagated by the CIA that the firstborn sons (once again, primogeniture!) from the middle classes and up were going to be sent to be indoctrinated by the communists. That rumor or something similar to it—perhaps without the detail of the firstborn, which was surely added by my parents to add drama to the matter—was the foundation of Operation Peter Pan. As its name indicates, the purpose of that operation was to encourage a relatively significant number of Cuban children (not only the firstborn males) to move north, where a series of sponsoring families would welcome them.

A rather sinister plan, it was nonetheless wrapped in a

supremely sweetened imaginary—as in the children's story from which the scheme took its name. Guided by the outstretched hand of a little green figure, the children would fly off toward Neverland while, increasingly diminished, the families of those children would be left behind until, finally, they would disappear. Things did not work out so benevolently, however, as is testified in the book *Waiting for Snow in Havana* by the historian Carlos E. Eire, a specialist in Calvinist iconoclastic movements in northern Europe during the sixteenth century.[7] In that book, Eire narrates his own saga as part of the plan conceived and implemented by the CIA in terms that are far from the cloying saccharine of the Peter Pan imagery. Personally, I was not a direct participant in these machinations, but my parents' decision to send me on my own to the United States was nevertheless not unrelated to the plan devised by the CIA, or the climate of unrest that was its main breeding ground. That was how, fleeing an imaginary danger, my father and I took a B-42 plane to Miami. Previously agreed upon by my mother and him, the idea was that my father would leave me there in the charge of a family whose patriarch was the main client of my father's law firm in Havana. My father would then return to Cuba. And that is how it happened.

Of this catastrophic mission concocted by my parents, my first memory is of the rattling glass windows in the brightly illuminated room of the Allison Hotel in Miami where my father and I stayed, buffeted by the winds of Hurricane Donna, which screamed and ululated outside. If I remember correctly, we arrived at his client's house the next day. The owners were an American Jewish family who had businesses in Cuba and divided their time between Cuba and the United States. For years before leaving the island, my family was a fixture at the bar mitzvahs and other celebrations and social gatherings at their home, and they, in turn, were regulars at the parties and festivities of my family. With the exception of their eldest son, who, when no one was around, managed to make my life miserable, I have only good things to say about them. The generosity with which, from the beginning, that family welcomed me still moves me. Unfortunately, I do not believe that they would have so many good things to say about me in return; to put it delicately, the terrified lost boy who suddenly descended into their midst from the sky was neither gift nor a miracle of myth.

To clarify the reasons for this asymmetry, I must briefly refer to what is at stake when one speaks of people's actions and initiatives. Generally, people talk about action in almost celestial terms, as something undertaken freely by a sovereign subject exempt from or uncontaminated by any corporeality. In order to understand how far reality is from this ideal, it is enough to take into account the experience of migration and exile—by which I mean that internal migration and exile that, until the great transnational migratory waves of recent years, has been the common experience of the poor in the Latin American nations. Far from the ideal of a subject operating in relative autonomy on the world, those who have gone through a thousand and one experiences in such situations know well how much acting and being acted upon are not sharply opposed phenomena. To the contrary: both dimensions are intimately linked in a game played to the death where, through the incessant flux of emotions, both terrifying and pleasurable, of drives, ingestions, digestions, and emissions, the body is a theater where the exchange between the inside and the outside is regulated. Nonetheless, when there is an overload of external forces acting on the body, the regulatory system that ensures this exchange between the inside and the outside sometimes breaks down. And when this occurs, subjected without filters of any kind to an invasive exteriority that destroys any proper place from which to act with a minimum of autonomy, people often either get stuck or even collapse. With all the floodgates razed and overwhelmed by an excessive emotionality that floods the interior uncontrollably, subjects simply fall apart.

Especially in the United States, where publications with this theme continue to appear, affect and emotions have been at the center of countless writings in recent years, particularly in the humanities, but also in disciplines such as anthropology. Without denying how penetrating and illuminating many of those texts undoubtedly are, my impression is nevertheless that this literature suffers from that excessive abstraction and overgeneralization to which García Vega, the Cuban writer, alluded in our conversations on the streets of Caracas in the 1970s. My sense is that the particular history, nuance, and intensity of my desperate efforts to hold my emissions "inside" for as long as possible would elude a general theory of affect. Such desperate and defeated efforts of self-control were evidenced by the piles of my dirty underwear in the corner of some closet in that family's house, piled up there by me in the vain hope that they would go unnoticed. I think that expressions like "shitting oneself with fear" allude precisely to situations like that, which literature is especially able to communicate. That is to say, situations of abandonment like mine manifested themselves with a singular virulence from the moment that my father left me alone with what was, to me, an unknown family, since it was my father (and none other) who left me destitute in their care.

For the ten-year-old child that I was, with a history and trajectory like mine, all the kindness and generosity in the world were not enough to mitigate the "strangeness" of my new accommodations. Faced with such strangeness, that child simply shat himself with fear—and this, despite the desperate attempts to contain everything, for as long as possible, without even venturing "outside" into that unfathomable "no man's land" to which, in any case, he had already entered and which had entered him even before he arrived at this new but foreign home. Confronted with that "outside" that, like a shadowy guest, had already taken up residence "inside," that child shat out of pure fear. It horrifies me to think what this poor family must have gone through with me, without ever, at any time, any of them making any mention or allusion to my "secret."

Although my memory of this time is that it lasted long, I am told that it barely extended to three months. The situation finally came to an end with the arrival of my mother, my older sister, and my brother, still a babe-in-arms, in Miami. By order of the Cuban authorities of the time, my mother left Cuba with only one Cuban peso in her bag. If I am not wrong, the Cuban peso and the dollar were roughly equivalent at that time. Something that the customs officers at the airport in Havana missed or did not take into account, however, was the much more valuable cargo that my mother managed to smuggle right in front of their noses. In fashion at that time, the beehive hairstyle permitted my mother to hide from the customs agents every jewel she could insert. Thanks to the sale of some of these jewels, later, when we had moved to Spain from Miami, it was possible to buy the old car with which we used to travel and some other things that I no longer remember.

As for my father, he stayed behind in Cuba for the time being. He had two reasons to postpone his exit from the island. Initially, he stayed with the thought of plotting against the new revolutionary government; then the denial of his asylum request by the US embassy in Havana convinced him that the Cuban authorities were about to arrest him. The embassy's denial was motivated by a dossier that had been in the hands of American intelligence for some time, identifying my father as nothing less than a KGB agent. His surprise when he found out the reasons for his declined visa must have been enormous. Indeed, considering my father's career, the situation could not have been more absurd. Far from any Stalinist flirtation, if my father was anything during his youthful years, he was, if not a militant, at least a sympathizer of the Spanish Falange. Moreover, if not for the whistle-blower who alerted my paternal grandfather to the danger, he would have stowed away at the age of seventeen on a merchant ship about to set sail from the port of Havana bound for Spain. His purpose: to join the insurgent or "Nationalist" side in the bloody civil war between "Nationalists" and "Republicans" that had erupted in Spain during the last summer vacation that my father took to Cuba to visit his parents, from Spain, where his mother's family resided.

Behind the imbroglio was my father's red aunt. Between the ages of seven and nine, my paternal grandparents had sent my father to France, supposedly to learn French, but in reality, to spare him the humiliation of the other students pointing him out as their illegitimate son. After two years with a French family, to which my paternal grandfather would surely have sent a remittance for housing and food, my father went to Spain to live in his mother's aristocratic milieu. With the exception of the trips he made to Cuba during the summers to visit his parents, between the ages of nine and seventeen years—that is, for about eight years—my father lived in Spain. I am sure that if it had not been for the fact that his paternal grandfather caught him red-handed when he was trying to stow away, he would have remained in that country, where, perhaps, his "faulty origin" would possibly have gone more unnoticed. Now that I think about it, compared to my father, my own abandonment saga would seem almost insignificant. No wonder that my mother used to repeat to me and my siblings that if we knew how much our father had suffered, we would forgive him many things. I'm not so sure about forgiveness, but the truth is that, as I reflect on the past from this moment, a certain compassion toward my father has been making its way into my feelings.

Be that as it may, what interests me is the way in which his Spanish stay throws light on the comedy of errors in which, much to his dismay, my father found himself suddenly transmuted before the eyes of the North American authorities into an agent of the KGB. Maybe because of the taste for symmetry—that, and the insistence to this day of the more rancid right in Spain, that the atrocities committed by the two sides in the civil war were comparable or equivalent— my parents used to say that, of the twenty-two people assassinated during the civil war in my father's Spanish family, eleven were killed by the Reds and eleven by Nationalists. These accountings seem to me suspicious, especially considering that the environment in which my father lived following his arrival in Madrid was overwhelmingly conservative. There was, however, my father's red aunt and her son who, in time, did come to serve as a well-known Soviet agent. Apparently (I was told), after the civil war ended with the triumph of Franco and the Nationalists, the red aunt went into exile with her son in Paris, but not before having taken with her some of my father's identity documents, though, at that time, he already resided in Havana. Once in Paris, this aunt did two things. First, she broadcast an anti-Franco radio program, which she directed herself. Second, she passed my father's identity documents to her son. Taking them for his own, from what I have been told for years, that son was able to act in the most varied scenarios as a Soviet agent, using my father's name and surname as alias. When my father decided to seek asylum in the United States embassy in

Havana, the result of his request had already been sealed in advance.

Returning to my mother and my two siblings, after their arrival in Miami, things changed drastically and not precisely for the better. To begin with, shortly after that arrival, I moved from the beautiful villa of my father's client in the Miami Beach area to a house in the dilapidated west of that city that my mother, my two siblings, and I shared with another Cuban couple whose boisterous expressiveness still echoes in my ears. Coming from a family where people generally didn't swear, the "damns" and "fucks" (*coños y carajos*) that often flew between these other Cubans were a novelty for me. If I'm not mistaken, the man worked as a construction contractor in the low-income housing developments that my father was promoting in Cuba just before the revolution arrived. I believe that our stay at the West Side house had a lot to do with his and his wife's willingness to host us for free. Considering that despite the relative ease and abundance of our life in Cuba and the fact that, like many others, my family left the island only with what they were wearing, I can think of no other way to explain our stay in that house.

I remember that home on Miami's West Side as a large, ramshackle shell of grayish wood planks and relatively uninhabited spaces. I see myself there, sitting on the floor of the bare main area of the house, absentmindedly contemplating for hours the meager activities that took place there: the corpulent mistress of the house occasionally coming and going on her way to the backyard, hugging some enormous bundle of clothes; some elusive cat quickly crossing the area; perhaps my mother melancholically sitting in a corner. In my memory, I am sitting on one side, leaning with my back against one of the very high walls of the very sad main room.

At a time when all children, both in Cuba and the United States, wore long trousers, I see absurdly short black pants, culminating in a worn black shoe, one of my bare legs extending out over the wooden floor; finally, my head is tilted slightly downward in profile. As I mentioned a moment ago, my only activity consisted of absently observing, for hours, the little goings-on in the central area of the house which, in my memory, was a spaciously barren no-man's-land. "Espaciosamente desangelada" is a Spanish expression literally translated as "spatially devoid of any angel."[8] It provides for me the summary image of the experience of exile as precisely that empty space, inexplicably unfinished and crisscrossed by a series of dispersed appearances that no one would seem to want or be able to claim.

It was in that vacuously contemplative attitude that one day an inspector sent by the Miami School System found me in his efforts to discover why I was not going to school. The situation had to do with the move from the villa of Miami Beach to the rundown house on the West Side. Another way in which that move was for the worse was that it took me from the fabulous public school on Treasure Island, in the Miami Beach area, where my first hosts had enrolled me, to literally nothing. Also worth mentioning among the changes for the worse was the desolation I felt when, with the arrival of Christmas, there were no family gatherings, no gifts, no Christmas tree, or anything of the sort. More ominously, confronted by so much absence, the realization that Santa Claus simply did not exist became, finally, inescapable. Quite suddenly, the desolate surroundings of the house on the West Side lost any air of transitoriness and instead assumed the unshakable contours of permanent reality: that void which, from then on, would be mine. In other words, without realizing what was at stake, the Christmas fiasco acted on me as a kind of catalyst. In retrospect, it occurs to me that those contours were revealed to me in all their nakedness as the soulless foundation that, regardless of any passing fantasy of mine or anyone else, or the inevitable changes of scenery, I would henceforth have to traverse. In other words: "Boy, stop your musing with pregnant birds and look at what you have in front of your two eyes, because that is, simply, what there is."

It remains to be said that the no-man's-land to which I have been alluding as a kind of experiential substratum is also a scene of appearances and disappearances. To say that such a place is a fundamentally inappropriable territory—a no-man's-land—is equivalent to saying that no stable identity could prosper there. After all, to speak of identity one must be able to claim as one's own some place of origin with which to identify as the fixed starting point of what one eventually becomes. In the absence of this type of attribution, what remains is an intensely relational space where the pure event happens, a combination of dazzling appearances, metamorphoses, and disappearances, unburdened by an obligation toward any origin (real or putative), and, consequently, the subject is left to be consumed in the very fire of its pure eventfulness.

Firm Land (Tierra Firme), Land of Grace (Tierra de Gracia), the Portable Country, the Oil Camp: under all these names, Venezuela, the nation that I eventually came to recognize as my own, also recognizes itself as an essentially inappropriable territory of incessant disappropriations and transformations. The monumentalized figure of Simón Bolívar floats, suspended above this space of wanderings, offering the only stable axis in an infinitely malleable universe. In his figure, I recognize the self-monumentalization that I first confronted in the signature and the speechifying that my father attempted to transmit to me as a child in Havana. It was the poet, García Vega, who first pointed out to me what he called the "marble hats" (*bombines de marmol*) that lined the streets of Caracas and that mocked the pompous elites for making monuments of themselves.[9] But this gesture can be seen whenever men or women, poor or rich, for whatever reason, pretend, either in Cuba or in Venezuela, to a position of state authority in public. This logic extends beyond the proliferation of the nation's monuments or, as brilliantly analyzed by Michael Taussig, the mediums of the María Lionza possession cult.[10] In this regard it is not coincidental that both Cuba (José Martí) and Venezuela (Bolívar) seem to possess the most numerous and perversely overreaching state cults in all of Latin America. But at least in Venezuela, to be effective, these performers must also supplement their pompous self-monumentalization with their agitated dancing as an indispensable gesture to the nation's formless, ever proliferating, figureless sociality, which remains excessive vis-à-vis, or even extrinsic with respect to, state monumentality. As I argue in my book *Dancing Jacobins*, a montage of monuments and dancing, these performances strive to govern the nation's unruly sociality by articulating it to the monumentality of the state.[11] Hopefully, later on, when I address the María Lionza possession cult, the meaning of this dancing will become clearer. In that cult, I see a malleability and plasticity that are in tension with the figure of the founding father and every fetishized figure of the state. But for the moment, I return to my childhood memories.

Some may be surprised to hear that a ten-year-old kid like me still believed in Santa Claus. I don't think "belief" is the word that best describes my attitude toward the character at the time. I think that the cunning with which many boys and girls as foolish as me protect the enchanted circle of their childhood, refusing to hear anything that could even remotely threaten it, better clarifies the determination with which, despite the evidence, I refused to let Santa leave once and for all. Be that as it may, what is surprising is that my mother did nothing to mitigate the blow or dissuade me of my illusions, insisting, for example, that the reindeer were on vacation that year. Or that, if Santa Claus was passing by the house on the West Side, it was because, with the dramatic changes in circumstances, we had simply missed writing to him. Hers was a most disconcerting ellipsis. I think that my mother's silence had something to do with that fact (already alluded to) that, in her best moments, she saw herself as Scarlett O'Hara openly contemplating the destruction left behind by the hurricane-force winds of the revolution. If, as incarnated by Vivian Leigh, Scarlett O'Hara was ultimately able to look squarely at the "reality" left in the wake of those revolutionary winds, then, looking resolutely forward, my mother, surrounded by her three children, could too. This, of course, without it ever occurring to her to take the opinions of those children into account, much less asking them for any opinion. Perhaps, if it is a question of survival, anything, even the most gruesome melodrama, will do. The problem is all of the order of collateral damage.

Once the matter of his identity had been clarified, shortly after we had moved into the house on the West Side, my father finally arrived in Miami from Havana, but not without first having been forced to change sites several times, from one diplomatic headquarters to another. It was finally at the Brazilian embassy where he received authorization from the North American authorities to enter the United States. Shortly after arriving in Miami came the decision that my mother, my two siblings, and I would go to Spain to live in Galicia in the ancestral house that my maternal grandparents had there, in a village near Santiago de Compostela. As my sister tells me, that decision was made at the urging of my mother, horrified at the prospect of having to reside in the United States without any of the comforts she enjoyed in Cuba. Meanwhile, my father stayed on, "counter-revolutionizing" in Miami, where he barely managed to survive with the meager three hundred dollars that some Cuban junta member in exile gave him each month, probably financed with American money.

The separation did not last long. The event that marked the end of my father's stay in Miami was the failure, on April 17, 1961, of the Bay of Pigs invasion, advised and financed by the US State Department. This failure was the signal for my father to finally leave Miami to join us at my grandparents' house in Galicia, without being particularly happy about the decision. Indeed, my father arrived in Spain in a bad mood, supposedly caused by having to leave Miami and his counterrevolutionary activities behind. However, the "true" cause of his discomfort was something else. As my mother would find out later through a letter that she found "by chance" among my father's clothes after we had already moved to Madrid, the real reason for my father's distemper was having been forced to end the affair he had had in Miami with my mother's best friend.

Deep down, my mother never forgave him. For my part, it seems to me that the distinction between "apparent" and "true" causes always oversimplifies things. Whatever the case, paternal anger is no simple fairy tale. I still remember the tremendous beating my father gave me one afternoon shortly after arriving at my grandparents' house in Galicia when he discovered a novel, probably by Walter Scott, at that time one of my favorite authors, which I kept hidden just under the schoolbooks that I was supposed to be studying.

This is a good place to clarify something about what I have said so far about my relationships with my parents. Until now I fear that my father's manqué authoritarianism and my mother's unbridled narcissism have been described in rather dark terms, as these appeared to be the dominant qualities in these relationships. However, I have also referred to the innumerable stories that my mother told me and that I listened to, fascinated. And to the long hours my mother spent teaching me to read and to write, or helping me with my schoolwork. My father gave me books. As I discovered years later, in my sessions with my Chicago-based analyst, Jeffrey Stern, this parental gift has always been of incalculable value to me, without my knowing it. Many of the intuitions developed in this text owe much to the conversations that, over the years, I have had with this psychoanalyst. But that is another topic.

Returning to my father: all his love for me was somehow condensed in the books that he gave me. This was how he knew how to express that love best. The heartbreaking thing, however, is that what he gave with one hand, he took away with the other. Consequently, these paternal gifts were like the pharmakon that Derrida speaks of in his writings on Plato: they were both treatment and poison.[12] Hence, upon receiving them, I hastily hid them, fearful on the one hand that paternal love would unexpectedly turn into punishment, revealing once again its poisonous and painful burden of violence. On the other hand, by hiding them, I surely sought to keep these books as close as possible to my body, as missives of paternal love addressed exclusively to me. When, in one of our conversations, my psychoanalyst pointed out the possibility that, when hiding the books in my pants, this desire to be addressed by my father was the hidden meaning of my activity, my long career as a book thief (which continued, and sustained my graduate student reading habits) dissipated as if by magic. I never stole a single book again in my life. I'm still ashamed I did it.

That's how love was in my family, very difficult but, like a kind of Krazy Glue, it never ceased to exist, uniting us all even during the most maddening dissensuses and distances. Although, in the case of my family, dispossession and violence from afar won the game, I think that in some paradoxical way that difficult love has sustained me—of course, always with a lot of help from others. To demonstrate this, I only need to think of close friends who were severed from their families. Nobody recovers from that easily.

Although at first glance it seems contradictory, there is another aspect of my family heritage that I would like to highlight. I am referring to the integrity, decency, and sense of equality that—let's say behind closed doors and certainly not without slippages—my parents strove to exhibit in their dealings with others. An example of this is the birthday party held for two consecutive years at the parents' house of one of my sister's classmates at the Sacred Heart School in Havana. While the first birthday was well attended by many of the schoolgirls, who came accompanied by their respective families, the same cannot be said for the celebration that occurred the following year. Apart from my family, almost no one was present on that second birthday. It all had to do with the skin color of the parents of the honored girl; in the local taxonomy, she was surely much darker than what was considered acceptable in an elite school like the one my sister attended. Even today, the image of that event exudes sadness for me: my sister's schoolmate with her father and mother, the three of them standing on the steps with the spacious main living room of the house in the background, and my parents and perhaps someone else tentatively gathered around them, without anyone really knowing what to say or do and everyone pretending as if nothing was happening. In my memory, the honoree wears a white party dress with a wide skirt, the father is dressed in a cravat and all the celebratory attire, and the mother wears an elegant dress with a jacket. The three stand out as very tall and extremely thin figures. The dark tone of the eyes and faces of each of the three members of the family group is the undoubted axis of the composition; from there, the three of them still look at me.

I am convinced that the presence of my family in that disastrous "second time" had a lot to do with a certain egalitarian ethos of my parents, restricted, it is true, to the behavior that one had to display in dealings with others, especially in public. (Wasn't it Marx who said that, although history always repeats itself, the second iterations were always farcical?[13]) I say especially in public because behind closed doors, in private space, things were more complex. Despite all the brutalities that I and my two siblings had to endure, I do not remember any occasion in which any of the maids in the house was subjected to any mistreatment by my parents. To the contrary, both of my parents, but especially my mother, never stopped teaching us about the importance of "treating everyone like human beings" (the expression is my mother's). I am, of course, aware that the good treatment of domestic employees in no way contradicts the exploitative regime to which they are subjected. Indeed, this "treatment" is usually part of the ideology intrinsic to the perpetuation of that regime. Thus, for example, my mother often professed the "love" she felt toward her subordinates while denying their most basic demands. When, however, I compare my family's treatment of its employees with the despotic manners I have observed in other families, I cannot help but think that there was some truth in the insistence with which my parents lectured us about the importance of treating everyone with the same standards, regardless of the differences of race or class that may have existed between them.

After all I have said, perhaps I do not need to clarify that my parents' egalitarian ethos in no way included, for example, the notion that Black people had the same right as anyone else to occupy the highest social positions. Far from it. I am sure that this possibility did not even cross their minds. Moreover, although I don't see either of them publicly insulting anyone, I can't imagine them participating in a celebration of a Black Cuban family. This ethos had the rather restricted scope to which I just alluded. In other words, the boundaries of my parents' egalitarian ethos were very well demarcated. That's not the only reason why I think it would be unfair to say that their sense of equality was merely superficial, inauthentic, or simply accommodating. Along with other instances that I still remember vividly, the presence of both of them at the "second birthday" of my sister's schoolmate, when the vast majority of possible guests were conspicuous by their absence, is testimony to the opposite. No matter how contradictory this may seem or actually is, my parents upheld the idea that, regardless of differences in race, class, or religion, everyone, without exception, is entitled to the same respectful treatment—within limits. That respectful treatment of others was an eminently ethical principle. I think that the almost crushing insistence with which my parents always stressed it to us is proof of the importance that this principle had for both of them.

So, against the grain of their other frankly toxic traits, the only way in which, at least to a certain extent, I can explain to myself the egalitarian impulses that my parents exhibited in their public dealings with others is by appealing to the immigrant condition of my mother's family, on the one hand, and on the other, to the fact of my father's bastardy. As for my father, I imagine that this condition must have made him especially sensitive to any of the numerous more or less covert rudenesses or misdeeds that surely took place on a daily basis in a society like Cuba's. Whatever its origin, along with all the bad, and no matter how diluted it may have been in the dark waters of the time, that ethos and the values associated with it are also part of my family heritage.

Far from being given only once, this is the inheritance that one must continually assume simply to go on living. In partial defense of my father's memory, I must also say that the Falangism of his youth in no way translated into any subsequent fascist fickleness. In the few writings that he managed to publish, he always showed himself to be a convinced democrat. It occurs to me that his way of reconciling his early Falangism with his later democratic convictions is not very different from that of many others. As in the case of a certain Spanish right today, that manner of thinking was to stupidly argue that, in Spain, Francoism represented a necessary phase of transition to democracy after the totalitarian threat represented by the Spanish republic. All this, of course, is nonsense. Neither did the republic ever pose a threat of totalitarianism nor was Francoism ever anything other than the darkest and most brutal dictatorship.

Not long after my father's arrival in Galicia, one of his friends from his Spanish adolescence arranged an offer for him from the Mangold Language Academy to be director of that Swiss institution's headquarters in Madrid. In response to this job offer, my father and mother moved to Madrid while my sister and I stayed temporarily at our grandparents' house, preparing to take the high school entrance exams under the tutelage of a local rural teacher. The idea was that, after taking the exams, we would go to Madrid to meet up with our parents there.

If I'm not mistaken, the year was 1961. In that academy, located in a large multistory building on Madrid's Gran Vía, they taught a variety of languages, from Russian to Italian to English. (Apparently, the academy no longer exists—at least my Google searches did not yield any results.) As if to add another turn of the screw to the comedy of errors that was my father's life under the sign of illegitimacy, all the employees of the Swiss institution other than my father and the language teachers—ranging from his deputy director to the humblest street sweeper—turned out to be members of the Spanish communist party, then in hiding. In fact, the deputy director of Mangold, José María Bravo, had been in the relatively recent past nothing less than the greatest hero of Spanish republican aviation, having shot down twenty-three Nationalist planes from the skies above the Republic. Surprisingly, my father and José María Bravo struck up a certain friendship. I remember him and his wife, Natasha Ulianova, visiting my grandparents' farm in Galicia, invited by my parents during one of the summers we spent there. Like something out of a Russian novel, according to my mother, Bravo's wife's name was too artistic to be true. Who knows? Meanwhile, I remember Bravo and his wife Natasha visiting our grandparents' farm in Galicia one weekend. I remember them as a truly charming couple.

Surely without the knowledge of the authorities in Switzerland, the transformation of the Mangold branch in Madrid into a covert branch of the Spanish communist party would have had to do with this organization's decision to use the language academy as legal cover for its operations. The idea would have been to gradually bring back some of its militants, who were exiled in the Soviet Union, to position them in various jobs within the Madrid branch, from the lowest to the most elevated. I think that the illegitimacy of my father's origin must have had something to do with the rather mad circumstances in which someone of his ideas could end up as director of an institution with such an unusual team of employees.

Not protected before the law by the guarantee that legitimacy of origin generally confers, this bastardy almost inevitably afflicted my father's identity with great fragility, exposing it without remedy to the kind of tremulous alterations and equivocal situations that others belonging to the same social stratum are more easily able to avoid. So it was that, not long after the fiasco with the KGB, like a clueless monarch ignorant of the forces that destiny has unleashed upon him, my father suddenly found himself, without knowing it, occupying the upper echelon of a domain that, from him on down, was populated by a multitude of enemy agents. I still remember the elegant anthology of the Russian poet Yevgeny Yevtushenko that was part of the collection of Soviet literature edited by José María Bravo and his wife, probably with Soviet money.

Then, family history becomes blurred. According to the family version, the relatively unexpected decision to move from Spain to Venezuela had to do with the fundamental disagreement between my father and the institution he had to direct. Along these lines, this move would have been motivated by the massive heart attack that, a few months before this new change of country, my father would have suffered as a result of a heated discussion about—what else?—politics, in which my father and José María Bravo would have been engaged. I don't know. In this fictional version everything fits together too perfectly: persecuted by the communists, once again, my father must quickly evacuate the scene.

In 1965 we were all very busy, both practically and emotionally, preparing for our departure to Venezuela. The decision to leave Spain was related to the job offer that a friend from his youth, not in Madrid but in Havana, made to my father to join a company he owned in Caracas. Although also of Spanish origin, this friend did not come from the conservative environment in which my father developed during his years in Spain. Far from it. Like my father, because the outbreak of the civil war at his friend's age of seventeen prevented a return to Spain, this friend and the rest of his family had also lived in Havana—only, unlike my father, as republican exiles. Even more, before the exile to Cuba, the father of my father's friend had achieved a certain notoriety in republican Spain as an author of adventure novels. I think that, on the one hand, the relationship between my father and his friend says something about my father's flexibility; on the other, it also reveals how, despite ideological differences, members of certain social classes somehow managed to come together. Once again, a Spanish friend from his youth lent my father a hand, although this time he had met the friend in Havana and not in Spain.

I do not want to close this discussion without referring to something that I previously overlooked, but that I think deserves to be mentioned. These relatives from Cuba arrived in Spain before us. When we arrived at our grandparents' house in Galicia, Aunt Haydee was already there with her three children: Adolfo, Jorge, and my cousin Haydelín, who would have been one year old at that time. It would not be long after that my uncle Adolfo, Aunt Haydee's husband and my mother's brother, whom I referred to before as a kind of redeeming figure within the family, would also arrive at these grandparents' house in Galicia. Noticing my inclination toward drawing, one of the first things my uncle did after his arrival was to buy me a set of pencils and notebooks in Santiago de Compostela, so that I could give free rein to my never-realized artistic ambitions.

Regarding my cousins Jorge and Adolfo, it would not be long after I arrived at the house in Galicia before I became the undisputed leader of the gang of three who spent the day running around between the cherry and the apple trees in the orchard at the back of the farm belonging to that house. Considering that both Jorge and Adolfo were much younger than me, that development is not very surprising. Conversations years later with my cousin Jorge in the United States, a country where he went with his entire family after the brief transit through Spain, were for me a revelation. It turns out that, in light of those conversations with my cousin, whom I love very much, it became clear to me that the image of my childhood that until then I had cultivated—as someone allergic to the exercise of power and always willing to help the weakest party of the classroom—at least required some retouching. By then, I would have been about ten years old, my cousin Adolfo was six, and Jorge was about four. Although we later disagreed on the elements of these conversations, in one of them, I recall urging him to taste fresh cow shit with the promise that if he did, he would be able to fly like Superman. In a memory that still moves me, my skinny four-year-old cousin's big sky-blue eyes emerge from a distant past to look into my eyes with a mixture of childish defiance and credulity. As he looked at me, he quickly licked with the tip of his tongue the end of the elongated twig that he held in his right hand after having tentatively driven it into the fresh dung that was lying near him on the ground. Jorge also alluded in those conversations to the time when, still in Havana, I plunged him in the salt waters of the Biltmore Club, bringing him back to the surface again and again in order to catch some air, only to submerge him again. I hadn't remembered that, although I did remember the times that other children older than me had made me suffer similar immersions.

In sum, one is part of a chain, as demonstrated by the fact that, shortly after arriving in Queens, my two cousins introduced a long series of children younger than them to the delicacies to which, not so long before, I had introduced them. A practical lesson that I learned from my cousin's anecdotes is how selective memory can be. Another lesson is that, despite the omissions, during my childhood, the robust joys of power had not eluded me as much I as had wanted to believe up until then. Living under the sign of Francoism, which, like a malevolent miasma, enveloped practically everything of my years in Spain before arriving in Venezuela in 1965, I will recount only the basics, generally limiting myself to the atmospheric.

As I have already mentioned, after my parents moved to Madrid, my sister and I stayed one more year in Galicia at our maternal grandparents' house, preparing with a local rural teacher for the high school entrance exam. After a year, in 1961, we went to Madrid to join our parents while, in one of those decisions characteristic of my family, my little brother was left behind in the care of his maternal grandmother (our grandfather had died more or less a year after we arrived in Galicia). Of the approximately four years that we spent in Madrid, I will mention, first, the Claret School, of the Claretian Brothers, where my parents enrolled me when they arrived in the Spanish capital, and the brutal beatings that the priests in black robes of that institution routinely inflicted on the students. At that time, corporal punishment was an accepted norm in the Spanish educational system. The lanky silhouette and yellow hair of one of the Claretian priests, an instructor, if I remember correctly, of Spanish grammar, continues to linger. I still see him with relative clarity, knocking one of the schoolboys to the ground with a single slap, and then proceeding to give him a series of swift kicks; and this, in full view of the entire room. A detail that, for me, summarizes the peculiar mix of systematicity and cruelty typical of the Claretian educational system is the priest's sharp-fingered right hand neatly rolling up his cassock just below the knee to allow his shoe to maneuver freely. Throughout the entire episode, the priest remained upright with his head tilted downward, looking down from above at the schoolboy bent over in pain on the ground, without, even for a moment, letting his rage take over, lest it decompose his perfectly controlled figure.

To round out what has been said about the Spanish educational system under Franco, it is enough to mention what, in a recent interview, the film director Pedro Almodóvar said about another educational institution of that place and time. In that interview, Almodóvar referred to his years at a boarding school for priests, this time not Claretian but Salesian from the provinces, in similarly intimidating terms. A "Big Brother of the beast," this is how in that interview Almodóvar summarized his vision of an educational system where, in his estimation, the sexual abuse of schoolchildren by priests was "the daily bread." I was lucky not to have been sent as a boarder to any of those "religious" schools!

Terror tells its own stories. At the end of the first school year, when classes had just ended and, like an infinite promise, summer vacation was just around the corner, I remember boasting to my parents that I had passed all my subjects. A few days later, the inevitable happened. Immediately after I arrived at the family apartment with a terrible sunburn, having spent an entire afternoon in one of those public pools with which Madrid residents try to mitigate the effects of the capital's terrible summers, I received the most unfortunate news.

As soon as I opened the door, Pepita, the maid who was working in the house at the time, let me know (at that time my parents had gone out) that that same afternoon my school report card had arrived and not only had I not passed the seven subjects corresponding to that school year, but, unfortunately for me, I had failed them all.

I remain convinced that when I bragged to my parents about my school achievements, I was being absolutely sincere. That's how self-persuasive fear can be! That day ended with Pepita in the waning light of the evening, smearing my body with balm to relieve my sunstroke while, in a low voice, she cautiously suggested that one day, I could do the same to her. I was so innocent that, not for a moment did I grasp the thinly veiled meaning of what she was proposing. By then, I would have been about twelve or thirteen years old and Pepita was around twenty. Without much formality, the next day at noon, standing in front of me, my father slapped me resoundingly, but not before having demanded that I stand firm with my hands clasped behind my back as I awaited punishment. Then, after closing the sliding glass door that separated it from the living room, he locked me on the small terrace of the apartment. Something happened there for which, to this day, I cannot find any clear explanation. Doubling over in pure terror in a corner of the sunny terrace, suddenly, without me looking for it, the unexpected happened. Hunched over on the terrace floor, my body was suddenly shaken by a succession of painful spasms that, without me doing anything to provoke it, culminated in the first ejaculation that I can remember.

To this day, this scene of initiation into adolescence, if that is what it was about, disturbs me. In its alchemy of pure terror and erotic automatism detached from fantasy or any provocation, bursting, once again, from the depths of terror as an uncontrolled emission, this scene strangely resonates with my tribulations at the home of my father's client in Miami Beach. Shaped under the sign of fear, the scene retrospectively prefigures the Gordian knot in which, until relatively recently and still—these things find a way to return where one least expects it—has consisted of the intimate tessitura of my experience. Woven of closely intertwined threads, premonitions, desires, physical emissions, and, later, writing itself, these images intersect in that knot which overdetermines and even merges as forms of action on the very threshold of that ominous no-man's-land governed by the patriarchal order that, in one way or another, we all, without exception, suffer. Neither men, nor women, nor children, nor nonbinary people, nor swallows nor insects: no one escapes from that order. As long as it persists, nothing and no one will be safe. Not even the constitutionally failed patriarchs or manqués like my father and all the others, all determined to embody an order that nonetheless always ends up costing them the proverbial pound of flesh. I think that any intuition I may have had about the meaning of forms of government and daily life, both in Venezuela and in other places, owes much to the fact that, given my personal trajectory, I have had no choice but to deal with the Gordian knot of the subject's constitution under patriarchy, in some way trying to undo it, or, at least, to loosen it. For me, this has been a matter of sheer survival.

But beyond any general consideration, one possible key to what happened on the terrace of the apartment in Madrid may be the fact that, located on a high floor of the modern apartment building where we then lived, that terrace faced the enormous redbrick monstrosity of the Claretian school, which extended several floors below. The fact of finding myself trapped, so to speak, suspended, at a considerable height on the small terrace of the family apartment between, on the one hand, my father, at that moment installed in the living room of the apartment from which only the sliding door separated me, and, on the other, the Claretians below, must have had something to do with the triggering of the crisis. "Between a rock and a hard place." Between a rock and a very hard place, this American saying sums up quite succinctly my situation on the terrace of the family apartment in Madrid.

After the first apartment in Madrid came a move to another part of the city, and, with it, a new school, also located right in front of the apartment where we moved, only, this time, the school was secular and much friendlier than the Claretian hell that I had left behind. Led by an elderly teacher whom I remember as a benevolent figure, this school was no example of academic excellence. Those were the years of the twilight of old-fashioned rock-and-roll and the arrival of the Beatles, and in that not very well-off middle-class environment, the most daring students in the room wore the famous bell-bottom pants of the time. A frequent activity after classes ended was to go to a nearby games room to play foosball, a game in which some of my classmates excelled as true masters. I remember this room as huge: beyond some pool tables, it was packed with foosball tables lined up in successive rows reaching all the way to the back wall. As one might expect, during my years in Madrid my transformation into the self-destructive and unruly teenager who imploded like a grenade somewhat later, on the streets of Caracas, was begun. For now, everything was limited to an increasingly catastrophic school performance, entire afternoons wandering around El Retiro park without going to class—either on my own or with some other high school classmate whom I barely remember—or, if not, trapped red-handed by the owner of some record store in Madrid with a 45 RPM record hidden like a fatherly missive in the front of my pants. It was around that time that my parents sent me for a summer as a boarder to the most punitive school in all of Spain, located near Santiago de Compostela in Galicia. When that happened, things were already so advanced with me that one of the most brutal caretakers at the boarding school at one point said that with one more like me, the school would have to install machine gun nests.

That was also the last time my father physically punished me. When, scared to death, I stood up to him with my fists raised, he simply backed away. At that time, I was already about fourteen years old and at least as big as my father. Unfortunately, my older sister was not so lucky.

Shortly after these events came the departure for Venezuela. According to what they tell me, one of the events that marked that departure were the heart-rending screams of grandmother Josefa when my parents picked up my five-year-old youngest brother after having left him living with her in Galicia for four whole years.

After the oppressive years in Spain, Venezuela was for me freedom. And that from the beginning, almost from our arrival at the port of La Guaira aboard a Spanish liner, the *Guadalupe*, one fine day in 1965. At least looking back, the promise of freedom unfolding in all directions, like a wind rose (or compass rose),[14] was already there, germinating in the human hubbub that greeted us at the docks as the *Guadalupe* came into port. Made up of customs inspectors, porters, loaders, stevedores, street vendors, and, surely, idle spectators, I dimly remember that feverish hubbub as a tide of sweating bodies, uncontrolled screams, and countless comings and goings under the tropical sun. From that memory, the dominant note is that of light invading everything.

The initial feeling of freedom was happily confirmed by the walk that, a few days after arriving, I took on my own from the apartment that my family rented in the El Rosal area, just one block from Francisco de Miranda. Starting from El Rosal, and always with the Ávila on one side, crossing block after block, first Chacaíto, and then Sabana Grande, this inaugural walk culminated well after the sun set on Plaza Venezuela, and ended in my encounter with an apparition. With the drone of the city as a soundtrack, and complete with its fountain of prodigiously dazzlingly illuminated waters flanked, on one side, by modern buildings crowned with illuminated advertisements, and, on the other, by the Eastern Highway, the Guaire River, and, beyond, the campus of the Central University, the square suddenly unfolded before my adolescent gaze. I was like Alice in Wonderland in a beautifully illustrated book, the prodigious wonderland that, free from the usual terrors, I would from then on navigate. Or at least that is how I recall my initial encounter with the square: with that sense of a sudden apparition.

After all these years, this inaugural vision of Plaza Venezuela has lost none of its initial allure. In my memory, it was not I who went to meet the square but Plaza Venezuela itself which, like a living creature, came excitedly to welcome me in all its twilight majesty, seductively commanding me to come out of myself. The world was no longer a wasteland; the square unfolded before me a fecund territory of unsuspected affects, sensations, and potentialities. Its promise could not have been more explicit: "as long as you manage to put your fears aside, from now on you will find in this square, and in all of Venezuela, a space conducive to any and all journeys, metamorphoses and transformations." As it has come to me over the years, surely as a composite of the various Plaza Venezuelas that have been established over time, that vision somehow persists as the incandescent core of all my returns and all my departures.

As the philosopher Jean-Luc Nancy suggests, emotions—above all those that are most formative for us—do not only move us from the outside and are not merely provoked by some external stimulus. Originating outside, emotions also shape us from within, in some way constituting the most intimate core of what we are, as long as we participate in a formless being-together impregnated with affectivity. I am of course writing about a vision of Plaza Venezuela from many years ago. In its intense emotionality, that vision illuminates my "inner dwelling" like a still-burning fire. In all its sensory richness and material abundance, that vision is for me the most powerful of emblems. Almost from the beginning, it operated in and on my subjectivity with a verily totemic force: a mysterious signifier gathering together the multiplicity of activity in a tentatively unifying image. Condensed in this all-encompassing image, the Plaza suggested that the formless "being together" in which I found myself involved from the very moment of my arrival was Venezuela. Or at least it was the other of Spain and Cuba. For reasons that are not entirely clear to me—the paths of the heart are to a certain extent inscrutable—this inaugural vision of Plaza Venezuela somehow allowed me to divine a differentiated collectivity in the shapeless and dispersed crowd in which I felt supported for the first time. Both in the emotional field and in the imagination, that unifying vision was my first apprehension of Venezuela as a nation relatively differentiated from the others I had known, giving me the "imagined community" with which I—finally!—could identify myself and to which I could affectively belong.

Perhaps a clarification is needed. Until now I have been using the words "emotion" and "to be emotional" (or "moved" and "moving") in their etymological sense of "motion" or movement in such a way that to "become emotional" or "to be moved" would imply being affected by an external agency. However, emotionality can also mean the opposite, if we place the emphasis on the subject of the movement, the one who is moved, and not on the external agency causing emotion. That is to say, despite disappointments, the initial vision that I had of Venezuela still excites me today. Needless to say, first impressions, if not necessarily misleading, are at least partial. Also, as in the scene of the ice water in the Havana apartment with which I began, promises and disappointments are often the obverse and reverse of the same coin, succeeding and replacing each other in an incessant relay. Things being what they are today, it is Venezuela in its promise, the promise of which I became a repository in my initial visit to the square, and not in the violence, caesuras, and prohibitions that are inherent to any nation-state, that moves me to this day. Despite the horrors and mistreatment to which this country has always been subjected, and especially in recent years, it is nevertheless that initial promise which, to this day, has not ceased to excite me.

As might be expected, after the initial exaltation, setbacks were not long in coming. On the one hand, my family relationships, which had already been degenerating since Spain, were brought to a crisis—so much so that my presence in the family became unsustainable. From that period, the image I retain of my father is not that of any prohibitive patriarch but of a man diminished by circumstances, going out every morning with a portfolio under his arm to sell promotional space and product placements for the newsreel agency that had hired him in Caracas.

On the other hand, my situation at the San Ignacio school, where my parents managed to enroll me shortly after our arrival in Venezuela, did not put me on a better path. If it had not been for my modest acting talents as a member of the San Ignacio theater company, I think that the Jesuits would have shown me the exit well before my final expulsion took place, barely a year after having entered. No more than a year and a half or at most two years had passed when I was already occupying a room in a rundown boardinghouse in the Sabana Grande area, subsidized with a small allowance from my family. This was supposedly to prevent the heart attack that, due to the continuous fighting, would have otherwise killed my father. What followed was a succession of adventures, some quite bizarre, to which I will not refer, except in passing, in what follows.

Before, however, there was Plaza Altamira. For a few months before I left home, this very elegant urban space—once again a square!—was my home away from home. It was visited every afternoon by a crowd of teenage prostitutes, the so-called *caminadoras* (streetwalkers). By then, my family had already moved from the initial apartment in El Rosal to one in Altamira Sur, just two blocks from Plaza Altamira. Just five or ten minutes of walking were enough to drastically change the scene, replacing the suffocating atmosphere of my family with a space of unpredictable circulations and hallucinatory images, or, at least, that's how it seemed to me. Given the possibilities, it would have been strange had I not succumbed to the manifold enchantment of Plaza Altamira. It was enough for me to receive news of what was happening there for me to be hypnotized by the spectacle that the square offered.

And what a spectacle it was! Emerging from who knew where to swirl around the benches of that urban space, the teenagers visiting the square each afternoon made of the scene an exuberant festival for my unsuspecting senses. Many of them in fact were no more than fifteen or sixteen years old themselves—about my age. Each day and without fail, it was as if the gaze that until then had only wandered through a gallery of grotesqueries (authoritarian parents, monstrous priests, abominable civil guards) now found itself displaced horizontally, beyond the confines of the gallery, into one of those motley popular festivals in the fields around Madrid that Goya knew how to paint so well. Like those Goya-esque festivities and spread throughout the square, the crowd assembled there performed an unbelievable display every evening. Very young women, or girls, wearing the hot pants of the time, would quickly spin the wheel of a lighter (probably Lido brand) to light a cigarette with incomparable savvy and sophistication, and then draw the smoke through their strikingly painted lips before blowing it out again. Everywhere there was laughter, gestures, looks, movements, and, from time to time, some young pimp pulling one girl or another aside, demanding that she account for herself.

There was also no lack of police raids. From time to

time, there suddenly arrived in the square groups of uniformed police determined to put the *caminadoras* into dully painted blue patrol cars, conveniently parked at the side of the square. For reasons of surely dubious romanticism, the image that first comes to my mind to convey the impression of these multitudes of girls (or young women), rushing north or south, from one corner to another of the square, with the uniformed police on their heels, are the flocks of starlings that I observed flying over the skies of Amsterdam some time ago. Moving back and forth at dizzying speeds, with the sun behind them, while drawing figures of implausible elegance in the sky, these singularly beautiful late-afternoon flights captured my still-living hope that in some possible world, these young women of Plaza Altamira continue to elude their persecutors. Not, then, "walkers," but, more accurately, swiftly flying birds, the "starlings" of my imagination. Even today those teenage visitors to Plaza Altamira appear in bold figures on the flagstones of the square.

Very much against the grain of the forced confinement to which I had been accustomed, what for me took shape every afternoon in Plaza Altamira was a liminal zone where everything established tended to blur, losing its usual contours. Far from any preestablished place or identity, there was something more interstitial in that square that lasted until late at night. Even if the situation I describe did not last but a few months before the "forces of order" finally managed to evict the "unwanted" visitors from the square, Plaza Altamira retained its reputation as an area where the most unusual encounters were a matter of course. Every day, every afternoon, something very different emerged in the square: not in the sites or the established identities, per se, but rather in the spaces "between" those sites and identities.

This is equivalent to saying that Plaza Altamira was a place open to the most prodigious metamorphoses and transformations. In the square, literally anything could happen. The powerful emotional currents that continually ran through the interstices "between" the looks, the gestures, the touches, and the sensations that, minute by minute, crossed there, left no one indifferent. No matter who they were, and as long as they did not come with the intention of controlling the place as a whole, as was the case with the police, the visitors to the square could not help but be changed by the unusual affectivity to which, whether they liked it or not, they were exposed there. Such transformations occurred irrespective of who those visitors were, from prostitutes and pimps to the most unsuspecting interlopers (my case). To experience the powerful currents of change that circulated in that place, it was enough to participate in the wondrous emotional network that was ceaselessly being woven "among" its visitors. In their spontaneity, the emergent affects and emotions that continually flowed through those intricate webs could not but be extremely powerful vectors of change. Once immersed in this affective torrent, already-constituted identities were inevitably subjected to a process of incessant reconstitution. For a few months, and almost as if by miracle, the Plaza Altamira of my memories was one of the most extravagant places imaginable, a place where, as in a pressure cooker at very high temperatures, the transformation of subjectivities occurred at accelerated rates.

What I have just said presupposes something essential. It is therefore important to note that, not only in the square but everywhere, far from being given, subjectivities have always been crucially formed and reformed by the experiences, affects, and emotions to which they are exposed. In this sense, the most that can be said is that, in its anomalous affectivity, Plaza Altamira only highlighted what has always been the case. What, then, would be the specific difference that distinguishes Plaza Altamira from those other scenarios, elsewhere? What, for example, authorizes me to suggest that the same subjects who entered the plaza imbued with relatively stable identities nevertheless left that enclosure substantially changed, penetrated in their identities by the alterity that they encountered there? If, both in the square and in those other places, affectivity plays a similarly decisive role in the formation and transformation of identities, what, then, would be that "X factor" that would allow one to be differentiated from the others?

The answer to these questions lies in the exceptional ways in which that affectivity, no matter how briefly, came to circulate in the plaza. If, unlike what usually happens in other settings, Plaza Altamira was for a time something like a vortex where all kinds of transformations routinely occurred, the explanation must be found in the Plaza itself. For reasons that elude me, during a fleeting interregnum, the emotional exchanges between individuals were not subject to the same type of regimentation that usually prevails in most other social spaces; hence the relative exceptionality of the place. While in those other spaces, that affectivity would be regulated by the state and other institutions from the top down, that is to say vertically, the same could not be said of what took place in the square. What transpired there during the brief months in which I was part of the tumultuous sociability of the place (before, that is, "the forces of order" managed to return it to "normality") was something very different: not the presence but the relative absence of any regimentation from above. At least as far as I was able to observe during that period, the sociability of the square was not subject to any vertical control. With all the caution with which the term must be used, whatever it may have been, the control that there was, was largely "horizontal" in nature. Always at risk of collapse due to an unforeseen turn of events, any precariously emergent form of control—for example, by young pimps over the "streetwalkers"—emerged from and was reaffirmed in the very exchanges between the visitors of the square. The results could not have been more significant.

To appreciate the consequences of such a relative absence of vertical regimentation, there is nothing more illuminating than to return briefly to the institutional places in Franco's Spain where my earliest youth was spent. If there is something that I hope became clear when I referred to institutions such as the family or the schools that I attended in that fortress of armored Christianity that was the Spain of that time, it is how much that fortification was united by the purest and harshest fear. That fear was the mortar with which its walls, partitions, subjectivities, and divisions were made and held together. In its absence, the fortification would have quickly collapsed. Without this terror, exercised daily, meticulously, and relentlessly, the governability of the subjects of the regime would have been simply unthinkable. For this machinery to persist in its work of shaping reality, all the institutions that were part of it, from the family to the school, through summer camps and other similar niceties, had to continually imbue these subjects with their identities, sensibilities, and behaviors on the basis of the most excessive terror.

Continuously transforming less cohesive realities into tremblingly responsible units before the law (of the father, of the school, etc.), that terror acted on these realities with a miraculously totalizing force. Like when I had to wait for my father's loud slap in the face, firmly upright and with my hands properly clasped behind my back. It doesn't matter if the fleeting subject of authority that I was then later decomposed into a series of involuntary ejaculatory spasms. This is how we lived in the terrifying universe of Francoism: back and forth from rigor mortis to emissions and so on in a potentially infinite relay. Unless, of course, those subjects more or less fully embodied in all their dominating, stupidly imperious corporeality the sadism constitutive of the regime. But to a certain extent, no one escaped the ultimately corrosive terror of the regime, not even its most faithful executioners.

The subjects' mimetic adoption of the models of behavior and identity dear to Franco's regime depended, precisely, on their ability to experience that terror as the abyss that would open at their feet if they evaded its mandates. That terror was the dark reverse of all the iconography of the regime. The supposed "love" of the masses that this iconography exudes—from the Caudillo to the Virgin of Covadonga, and so forth—is nothing but the sanctimonious obverse of fear. That love was like whistling in the wind: a way to ward off the panic that truly united the masses with Francoism, and, above all, with Francisco Franco, leader for the glory of God. Chavismo's slogan, "Love is repaid with love," follows those same paths.

There is, however, a condition that must be satisfied at all costs if terror and the other affiliated emotions (guilt, shame, the sadistic aftertaste of power's exercise, and so on) are going to achieve their objectives; that terror and those emotions must be inculcated as vertically as possible, and to the maximal extent unilaterally, from top to bottom. This implies that for this work of inculcation to obtain results, the established powers must continuously strive to isolate subjects from any "external" influence capable of removing them horizontally from a relationship of continuous availability to the mandates and interpellations that come from above. In other words, to be successful, the institutions of Francoism had no choice but to constitute and reconstitute these subjects as monads uniquely responsible to its dictates, and, as such, hermetically sealed against all horizontally emanating emotional contagion from outside. For this, nothing but the most immeasurable terror was enough. Without the perpetuation of this emotional economy that links subjects to institutions through fear, simultaneously isolating them from their environments as hermetically self-contained monads, these institutions would simply vanish in the blink of an eye.

Nothing is further from this emotional economy than the Plaza Altamira of my adolescence. It is precisely this vertical economy that was suspended at Plaza Altamira for a few short months — although not necessarily without risks (other kinds of violence, including sexual violence against women, could also occur there). Relatively absolved of any affective "mandate" vertically induced by the established institutions, the visitors to the square briefly allowed themselves to be pulled — formed, deformed, and reformed — by the horizontality of their encounters. Instead of the vertically imposed terror, what took pride of place in the square, afternoon after afternoon, was the emotionality that flowed horizontally "between" those visitors, unpredicted and unpredictably emerging in the heat from their many encounters beyond any instituted discipline. In that fecund territory, discrete individualities did not prosper.

Instead of any individuality petrified by fear, what briefly traversed Plaza Altamira was something different. Imbued with an excessive alterity, what filled the square during that brief period was the "singular plural being" (as Jean-Luc Nancy describes it) of its visitors, which was emerging in all its singularity from each of the intrinsically plural encounters that wove these visitors together across the length and breadth of that urban arena.[15] I say plural because even in the most fleeting encounters an irreducible plurality intervened: from the time of day, to the prevailing light, whether or not there was wind or rain; to the smallest gestures, the clothing worn or the emotional temperature that, for one reason or another, contingently circulated among and shrouded these visitors. Absorbed by that enveloping skein, like one more of its circumstantial knots, the intimate being of those visitors incessantly mutated as they were "touched" by the emotions, sensations, and changing affects typical of the excessive relationships at the scene. It could well be said that, far from being given, the intimate being of each visitor continually emerged in its singularity from the plurality immanent to each of the multiple encounters that were taking place, minute by minute, in the plaza.

Thus, the intimate being of my fifteen-year-old self was swept up in the emotional whirlwind of Plaza Altamira. Emotionally assaulted in all directions by a veritable torrent of provocative glances, emotional insinuations, unusual images, or hitherto unforeseen situations, how could I not experience a significant mutation in everything that until then had been immovable for me? The very edges of what had been my world, with all its unbearably heavy and heartrending identities, could not help but break down at contact with the square. What, for example, it had meant for me to be a man or a woman was reconfigured by the expectant gaze of a girl more or less the same age as me, who, for a few brief seconds, indecisively stopped in front of me in a southern corner of the square, her eyes inquisitively fixed on mine before once again rejoining the crowd of her companions, who were running about us, pursued by flocks of uniformed police officers. Stopped at that threshold and assailed from all directions by these manifold new impressions and emotions, what was left for me but to allow myself to be reconstituted by the network of unexpected relationships in which I now found myself fatefully immersed?

Eroded by the intense emotionality that spread among its participants, including me, no prior belief could emerge unscathed from that square. The authoritarian parents and ignominious priests of my early youth in Spain ceased to be the only models of possible masculinity. In their place, the gallery of teenage pimps, self-absorbed poets, or sleepless chess players who frequented the square vied to replace them. As for my vision of the feminine, the pious aunts and the impressively dolled-up ladies of my previous life had no choice but to jockey with the versions of femininity appearing in the square. It was impossible to escape the moving mix of defiance and helplessness that emanated from their bodies and their attitudes, and that flowed "between" them. Allowing oneself to be overcome by that emotionality was to mimetically access versions of the feminine that, far from being bottled up or kept at bay, brought subjectivity closer to an unknown vulnerability. As in Baudelaire's poem about the Parisian masses, the funambulesque variety of the characters who hovered in the square offered a multiplicity of types ready to be mimetically appropriated, even if only fleetingly. As one allowed oneself to be infected by this lateral affectivity that emanated from each of these figures, whether it was the reckless audacity of some or the somnambulant intensity of others, it was possible to briefly inhabit possibilities of being, feeling, and acting that went beyond the authorized repertoires.

Thus, in addition to freedom, Venezuela was also the multitude for me. As I reflect, it becomes clear to me how much, from my arrival at the port of La Guaira on, my experience of Venezuela was marked by the experience of the urban masses and their uncontrollable proliferation. In a sense, my encounter with Plaza Venezuela was already marked by this proliferation, with the illuminated waters of its fountain, the winks of its glittering advertisements, or the continuous traffic of vehicles circulating around the fountain before moving off in all directions. Looking back, it is, however, in Plaza Altamira where the experience of the rural and urban masses, such a persistent key in my understanding of Venezuela, become recognizable. My later writings about the country provide a testament to that centrality. Considering that I came from a place like Franco's Spain, where any unauthorized gathering of individuals was strictly prohibited, it is not difficult to understand that, for me, Plaza Altamira was a revelation. It is enough to contrast the masses carefully orchestrated around the leader by the Franco regime, with the (to me) unprecedented proliferation of Plaza Altamira, to grasp the reverberations of this urban area throughout my subsequent development. While what predominated in the Spain of Franco was the mass ornament of which Kracauer writes,[16] carefully choreographed from the heights of power, what happened in Plaza Altamira was something quite different. What emerged there from this circulation of emotional excess was not, then, the mass as ornament, which is an artifact of power under conditions of industrial capitalism, but rather the mass as an intrinsically democratic entity, continually emerging from relatively spontaneous encounters between individuals. This ability to instigate change has tempted some to assimilate mass sociality to social movements. I think, however, that it is important to resist that temptation. Thus, while social movements of a classic type are generally articulated around a series of discrete demands addressed to the state and/or a centralized power that presupposes a unified subjectivity contemplating the future as the teleological realization of the demands and objectives of the movement in the present, none of this has anything to do with the type of mass sociality to which I have been referring. If anything should be clear, it is how much the changes induced by this sociality come about in unpredictable ways as a result of the energies that incessantly circulate "between" the subjects, and not as a result of the deliberations of any subject or subjects taken in their isolation.[17]

Thus, not only freedom and the urban masses, Venezuela was also democracy for me. Several authors have linked the experience of the urban masses since the industrial revolution with the experience and reality of democracy itself. Thus, for example, for Catherine Malabou, the modern urban mass is inextricably associated with this political form and is far from being a space of fusion where all distinctions are obliterated in a great undifferentiated whole. And contrary to what a certain fascist imagery proposes, left to itself, without any interference from above, the mass is a shapeless territory in continuous expansion where the "touch" (between bodies, gestures, glances) does not give rise to an undifferentiated amalgam but rather to a relationship of relative detachment between its participants. It is in this relationship of simultaneous contact and distancing that, according to Malabou, democracy is inscribed as a political form in which, far from being prescribed in advance, identities are susceptible to being mimetically adopted by subjects in a potentially infinite game of masks.[18]

Unlike what happens in authoritarian regimes, as, for example, in European absolutist monarchies or the Indian caste system, where what one is—noble, warrior, or saddler—is dictated in advance by the corporate group into which one was born or to which one has been assigned, things happen differently in a democracy. There, what a subject is or can become need not obey any previous script. In principle at least, the identities that are available at any time in democracy are available to everyone; in principle they can be mimetically adopted by anyone. And this, regardless of the race, social condition, or gender to which one previously belonged or was assigned.

This means that, in democracy, anyone can, in principle,

become, for example, president, pilot, artist, or engineer. Even identities such as being a man or a woman, which, until not long ago, were considered immutable and dictated by nature itself, can now, in a movement that some have hesitated to characterize as the expansion of democracy, literally be adopted by anyone. For such an adoption to be properly democratic, however, it must not be governed by any irresistible force compelling subjects to affectively merge with the models of identity offered by power. This is why Malabou, in a critique of Elias Canetti, insists that the "touch" of the masses in modernity entails fusion and distance at the same time: if fusion makes it possible to identify mimetically with the figures or types that one encounters daily, it is in the tacit distance in each of these identifications that the minimum of reflexivity resides, making it possible to play with different identificatory possibilities without being fatally tied to any of them.[19] For example, in Baudelaire's poem mentioned above about the Parisian urban masses, the poet is a kind of wandering spirit capable of possessing at will the different characters he encounters in his meanderings through the streets of Paris, inhabiting them provisionally without, however, definitively attaching himself to any of them.

Or, without going any further, there is my own example: my adoption of the different identities that came my way in Plaza Altamira. Not only did that adoption not entail any magical conversion process, but in the mimetic relationship with the others in the square, there resided the reflective distance that to a certain extent allowed me to access their alterity and at the same time play with the differences between the known and the unknown, the identities that until then had formed my personal repertoire and those that continually approached me in the square. From such play, nothing could emerge identical to itself. This play and the emancipatory possibilities that it entails are among the distinctive attributes of democracy. How different all this is from the situation in the Cuba of my childhood or in the Spain of my early youth! It is not incidental that both periods were presided over by two dictatorial regimes, that of Batista, in Cuba, and that of Franco, in Spain.

In my memories, the Plaza Altamira episode culminated with the interminable party that a friend of mine, who at the time called himself Douglas, threw in a recently vacated apartment, precisely in one of the buildings that overlooked the Plaza. Taking advantage of the fact that, after his father had moved from this apartment to another in the Palos Grandes area, there were still several days before the leasing agency would take charge of the place again, Douglas literally opened his doors to the entire population thronging in the square at that time. It was a typical gesture of his excessive taste for provocation. For three days the place where my friend's father had resided was the scene of an unlikely celebration: prostitutes, often accompanied by their clients, spread out in groups along the entire width and length of the large main hall, many with their bundles of clothes on hand; a continuous coming and going of the most diverse people inside and outside the apartment; one or another young pimp slapping his "protegé" in the hallway that led to the apartment; outraged neighbors accompanied by uniformed police officers surely seeking to identify the person or persons responsible for such an incident.

It was as if, suddenly, any distinction between the outside and the inside, the public and the private had resoundingly collapsed, with the unbelievable exterior that in the previous months had filled the square afternoon after afternoon finally breaking into the interior of one of the elegant buildings bordering the place. Although I don't know the details, I wouldn't be surprised if the party organized by my friend was the final straw that ultimately led to the square being cleared of its officially unwanted visitors. Curiously, my memory of the party is devoid of joy. In its desolate spaciousness, the vast unfurnished living room of the apartment my friend's father had just vacated did not differ too much from the central area of the house on Miami's West Side. As in that house, the main living room of the Altamira apartment was a large barren area, a no-man's-land where, like a gray sediment, an enormous sadness covered everything: from the mattresses erratically distributed everywhere to the bundles of clothes, coffee strainers, and groups of men and women scattered separately throughout the place. Of the carnal trade that surely took place in the apartment, the only thing I remember is my encounter on the tiles of the living room with the young woman with whom, during a brief interval, I had exchanged glances in one of the corners of the square. As for this failed encounter, my first attempt at having a sexual relationship, there is not much that needs to be said other than mentioning the gonorrhea that was the outcome of the experience, even though nothing was consummated there.

I think that the abysses of exposure and vulnerability that unexpectedly opened up inside a building that had been conceived precisely for the opposite purpose—that is, to protect its inhabitants from the inclemencies outside—say a lot about the country that Venezuela has been since the founding violence of the wars of independence. But let's proceed in stages. For now, I merely want to foreclose any temptation to find some sort of "ultimate truth" concerning the nature of the activities of the square in the zone of provisional exile where, for a few days, an unoccupied apartment became the stage for the predestined end of the exuberant masked ball of Plaza Altamira. I prefer to think of the relationships between the exuberance of the square and the desolation of the apartment not as if one were the truth of the other, but rather as transitory incarnations of the country's democratic promise, on the one hand, and, on the other, the mistreatment and disappointments to which this promise has been subjected in the midst of violence, abuse, and the inequalities that, until now, have been endemic to the history of the country. That promise and those disappointments run through both the history of Venezuela and my passionate relationship with the country. Perhaps due to narcissism on my part, I think of my relationship with Venezuela as an acute case of so-called elective affinities.

Shortly after what I have just relayed, my departure from my parents' house occurred, but not without being preceded by the prophetic words of Máximo who, to this day, remains one of my dearest friends. Now that I think about it, after my childhood friends in Havana, Venezuela also meant friendship for me. Other than Jesús, a Spanish first cousin of mine from my years in Franco's Spain, I cannot remember a single friendship from that interlude that deserves the name. But returning to my friend, Máximo, he, like me, frequented an *arepera*,[20] Tostadas El Cañón, located on one of the corners facing the southern area of Plaza Altamira. I remember him occupying a table near mine on the open-air terrace of the *arepera* accompanied by an older man and an American woman much younger than him, whom he was divorcing. I recall the three of them engaged in intensely lively discussions.

About eight years older than me, the Máximo I remember from that time was a terribly romantic figure. Around dusk, every afternoon without fail, Máximo went to the *arepera* dressed in black, accompanied by a German shepherd that lay meekly at the foot of the table while he and his two companions engaged in their lively dialogues. In previous years, Máximo had achieved a certain notoriety as an actor in the Ateneo de Caracas. He eventually abandoned that profession for reasons that have never been very clear to me. Something that, however, never abandoned him after his time in acting was a certain stage mastery, that indefinable quality that certain individuals, generally politicians or actors, possess to project an image of themselves that exceeds the limits of the merely human. It wasn't long after seeing him at the table with his vivacious companions before Máximo and I sat down to talk at one of the *arepera*'s outdoor tables. In one of those conversations, after expressing my fears related to my possible departure from my parental home, Máximo responded. "Don't worry, the night will provide." These words, spoken without blinking as he stared into my eyes, sealed what was to come. After nearly six decades, the deep resonance of my friend's warm voice still resounds in my ears.

Taken literally, Máximo's words do not remotely describe the thousand and one calamities I went through after leaving my parents' house behind. In a more poetic sense, though, those words did turn out to be prophetic. In likening the night to the prodigality of the maternal womb, Máximo captured something essential of my experience in the streets of Caracas after having left home. Spent under two dictatorships, the years prior to my arrival in Venezuela were decidedly dominated by the sign of the patriarchal. The same could not be said, at least not so unequivocally, of my time in Venezuela. Venezuela was something else. Although not without ambiguities and complications, if Cuba and Spain were the Father's reserve, then the territory of affections, experiences, and emotions that opened up to my experience as soon as I left behind the family home in Caracas was more of a maternal phenomenon. In line with certain authors, this territory could well be called "The Mother," as long as it is not apprehended in itself as a self-sufficient essence (or a biologized reproductive metaphor) but rather in constitutive tension with the state.

This polarity is something like that which structures the María Lionza / Simón Bolívar relation in the Venezuelan political imagination; the first figure of this dyad is the deity who presides over a spiritual possession cult with numerous adherents throughout Venezuela, and the second is the "founding father" of the country. At least from 1873 onward—when the cult of the founding father was first instituted during the regime of Antonio Guzmán Blanco—Simón Bolívar has unequivocally symbolized the republican state with everything it has to offer: founding violence, patriarchal will, and centralizing hubris. In her figuration as a celestial queen, María Lionza is, by contrast, a kind of hybrid between an Indigenous deity and a Catholic Virgin Mary. In that imaginary, she emblematizes a prodigious Venezuelan sociability in all its intense relationships and metamorphic potentiality. The selection of María Lionza as an emblem of the country's sociability is in itself a strong indication of how much that sociability is thought of and experienced by Venezuelans under the sign of the feminine. It is not for nothing that the claim that the country is a matriarchy is almost a cliché in Venezuela.

I am aware that I am treading on dangerously slippery territory here with the possibility of giving in to the most harmful stereotypes. About five decades ago, in 1975, a singularly malevolent little book was published in Venezuela titled *The Revolution of Intelligence,* which blames the supposed lack of discernment of the Venezuelan population and many of the country's ills on the matriarchal nature of the society. According to this book, the cause of all these evils would lie in the powerful influence that mothers exerted on the family environment and the formation of children in Venezuela.

To amend the situation, what would be needed, claimed the author, would be to restore the paternal figure to its rightful place of honor. All the chaos, informality, irregularity, and imbalances that supposedly affect Venezuela would be miraculously overcome once both the state and families returned to the patriarchal order that nature has always dictated. A topic frequently addressed in conversations in Venezuela is the lack of modernity that supposedly afflicts the country. When this topic arises, it is not uncommon for someone to attribute this lack to the marginal place that fathers occupy in family units, generally presided over by the maternal figure. In this discourse, once the necessary correctives are introduced, Venezuela will finally become the nation of virtuous men to which it was promised by the founding fathers, the community presided over by exemplary citizens of a certain republican imagery, all possessed of an unfailing righteousness and with unquestioned power over both the state and the family. Frequently invoked by historians of the Venezuelan nineteenth century, the notion of the state as a school designed to facilitate the access of the barbarian masses to citizenship is an intrinsic part of that manly republicanism.

Instead of clarifying anything, by putting the proverbial cart before the horse, what this type of speculation does is to obfuscate the situation. Looking at things more closely, at least from my perspective, one can see that, far from being the cause of any evil, the fluidity, malleability, porosity, overflowing affectivity, and absence of rigid borders that are typical of Venezuelan sociability have historically been a remedy (and source of strength). Over the years, that sociability has tried to protect itself from the many malignant forces that, in all their patriarchal violence, the exacerbated statism of local republicanism has unleashed in the country since independence. It is a case of "society against the state," to use the title of a now-classic little book by the late French anthropologist Pierre Clastres.[21] In fact, if we are talking about apportioning blame, then I think that the entity largely responsible for the many intractable problems that afflict the country is none other than the type of republican state that was first devised by Simón Bolívar in the heat of the struggles to withdraw Venezuela from Spanish rule. Later, in the last third of the nineteenth century, that state form and its axioms, fantasies, and bigotries were codified by the dictatorship of Antonio Guzmán Blanco and his Cult of Bolívar. The Chavista/Madurista state that, unfortunately, we Venezuelans have suffered for more than twenty years is little more than the latest "leftist" incarnation of this Bolivarian state.

But those are themes already developed in my book *Dancing Jacobins*. Here, I would like to briefly refer to some incidents that marked my foray into the domain of "The Mother," which phrase I use, following Jean-Luc Nancy and Philippe Lacoue-Labarthe,[22] to refer to the ineffable territory of Venezuelan sociability that I encountered after leaving my father's house behind. To summarize, "The Mother" of my recollections was a locus of prostitutes from the interior of the country, single men, provincial students, night owl poets, and outright rogues who were ready, at the slightest opportunity, to undertake acts of the most overflowing generosity. Unfortunately, narrating in detail my adventures and misadventures in that unconquered territory would not only be an interminable exercise, but even more problematic, it would unnecessarily distance me from the central objective of this text, which is to situate my writings about the country in relation to certain main lines of my life trajectory in Venezuela.

Suffice it to say that my first excursions into that domain of the feminine beyond my paternal home took place in a boardinghouse in Sabana Grande, which was inhabited mostly by prostitutes from the provinces. There my first relatively successful sexual encounter took place, precipitated by the "Let's go, *zingar papi*" that, with a mischievous smile, a woman I shall call Sonia addressed to me upon returning to her room, where she had locked me up, all her generous humanity wrapped in a tiny towel. The meeting was not repeated. I'm sure that the whole thing had much more to do with a certain compassion on her part for the beardless and slightly pathetic boy that I was then, than anything else. The fact that the incident was not repeated would seem to confirm this suspicion. After all these years, I am still grateful to her. Although she was Venezuelan, Sonia spoke in the purest Havana accent. Who knows if she had ever read Cabrera Infante, the novelist par excellence of Havana nightlife. This would not be implausible, considering that, although I never saw her again, I learned several years later from a mutual friend that Sonia had spent several years in Cuba because of her ties to the Cuban Revolution. In short, whatever else she might have been, Sonia was not, after all, any sex worker recently arrived from the provinces.

Then came the events to which I refer below, without adhering to any strict chronological order. First, the occasional encounters with the daughter of a French/Venezuelan poet determined to retrace the itinerary of her father, who would have spent part of his youth in the twenties or thirties in Caracas. She was constantly accompanied by a string of young men whom she diligently indoctrinated in "amour Bolivarienne pour la patrie" and the sacrifices that that love infallibly demanded. At that time, she (the daughter) would have been around thirty or thirty-five years old, although the estimates one makes in adolescence are never reliable. Then came my friendship with Arturo, the first homosexual friend I ever had, with all that this entailed for my confrontation with other ways of exercising masculinity. And then there was my passage through the pseudo-hippie magazine *Haoma*, edited by Andrés Boulton, the famous author of the book *The Orgasm of God* (at that time the orgasms that worried me were decidedly more sublunary). Shortly after we met, Andrés invited me to reside in one of the rooms at the magazine's premises located at the intersection of Chacao and Sabana Grande. At that time, he would have been around thirty or thirty-five years old. From that time, I recall my long-distance infatuation with the Maracucha writer Matilde Daviú, and my nightly trips to the El Viñedo restaurant in Sabana Grande, where at that time a good part of the Caracas bohemia gathered. I would go there in the hopes of bumping "by chance" into Matilde.

At some point, Andrés Boulton asked me to write a report on the situation then faced by *Imagen de Caracas*, the multimedia show created by the painter Jacobo Borges. *Imagen de Caracas* had recently been closed down by the Caracas government, which had accused Jacobo and his team of offering a tendentiously Marxist version of the country's history. It was 1967, and I was seventeen years old. When I first approached the premises where the show was supposed to be running, accompanied by Catherine, an Englishwoman with whom at that time I was semi-tied, I encountered a panorama that exceeded my wildest expectations. When I arrived, I found Jacobo and a large group of *Imagen de Caracas* workers camped outside the venue, demanding its reopening. For me, seeing the workers' tents was a dream come true. In those days the Berkeley student protests enjoyed a lot of attention in the media. The enthusiasm with which I dedicated myself to making out with Catherine between the tents was surely related to our belief that these acts incarnated the spirit of student rebellion that we imagined to be rampant on American campuses. The first suspicion that perhaps I was the victim of a mirage occurred when Jacobo took me aside and, in a tone of voice somewhere between serious and sarcastic, told me with feigned gravity, "Rafael, look, this is not Berkeley. Otherwise, it's perfect." The second such occasion took place after the evening reading of a poem of mine before an audience of the show's workers. "Red lions roar around my vital ectoplasm" was how the little poem just published by *Haoma* magazine began. Almost immediately after the reading, Jacobo took me aside to warn me about the inappropriateness of referring to the redness of the aforementioned felines in that place. It didn't take long before I realized that something similar to what happened at the Language Academy that my father had directed in Madrid was taking place in *Imagen de Caracas*: even the street sweepers there were in the communist party!

Any further possible misunderstanding on my part was finally dispelled when, crossing Francisco de Miranda with Douglas and I, Jacobo narrowed his eyes and told us in a mixture of sass and Caracas charm, "Do you want to shit yourselves? I'm a member of the communist party of Venezuela." Beyond the initial confusion, the "shitting ourselves" that was meant to happen didn't last long. It wasn't long before Douglas and I were participating in a three-way reading group with Jacobo. Althusser, Galvano della Vollpe, Gramsci, among others, were the authors whom the three of us discussed over the subsequent months. During that period, I was in charge of "expropriating" three copies of whichever author we were going to discuss from one of the bookstores in Caracas, and of sending a copy to each of the other two readers sufficiently in advance for them to read it before our next meeting. Quite an education, that!

It can well be said that, without completely abandoning the regions of "The Mother," my mature years began right there, in the ambiguously patriarchal territories of the Venezuelan left. I say "ambiguously" because, unlike other places in Latin America where I have had some contact with the local left (I am thinking of the Andean countries in particular), in Venezuela the situation is a little more complicated. Without denying the pernicious vernacular machismo and authoritarianism that, in line with the rest of the Caribbean, the Venezuelan left exhibits, it also displayed the same tendencies toward hybridization and the mutual contamination of the feminine and the masculine that characterized the rest of life in the area. But I don't want to exaggerate. Often that tendency toward hybridization only makes things worse.

What I mean is that this hybridization often provokes precisely the opposite tendency: indiscriminate violence eager to eradicate any possible ambiguity. It also encourages the molding of one's own identities and those of others as grotesque instantiations of masculine ideals. I must clarify here that in what I've just written, I was not thinking about Jacobo, but rather about the landscape that he put before me. It is true that Jacobo was an emblematic figure of the Venezuelan left, and, as such, it is impossible that he escaped all of its determinations (the same is also true of myself during those years). However, as the great artist that he was, Jacobo's relationships with these determinations were, to say the least, complicated, and he was always engaging them in a tacitly deconstructive spirit. Both in his painting and his personal life, he expressed his radical democratic sensibility in his relationships with others, including women.

Years later, Jacobo reminded me of the dynamics of our book club in front of a fairly large audience. Just after my wife, Patricia; Rigoberto Bastidas, a beloved Venezuelan friend; and I had said good-bye to Jacobo following an exhibition of his at a gallery in a villa in Caracas, he asked us to stay for a while. "Psst, psst, don't go yet," he urged us, while gesturing for us to hold on with his open right hand briefly suspended in the air. Immediately afterward, Jacobo went with us to the garden in front of the villa and right there, in front of all those who at that moment were chatting outside with their respective whiskeys, he began to refer with that sly smile of his to our shared readings from those many years ago. And Jacobo devoted special attention to those occasions when—"Chas!" [voilà]—I put a stolen book—or as Douglas liked to say, a "justly reclaimed" book—in his hands. To this day I wonder what the well-dressed visitors to the gallery must have thought of that cocktail-party effrontery to local bourgeois sensibility.

I don't remember if it was at the same time or shortly after the reading group stopped meeting that I worked for a time as a night receptionist at the Capri Hotel on one of the parallel streets to Francisco Solano, in the vicinity of the Grand Café on Sabana Grande. At that time, the Capri was a hotel occupied exclusively by a diverse group of prostitutes from the provinces. Despite my brief initiation by Sonia, my profound shyness in carnal matters was far from having been overcome; to me, sexuality was still one of those unfathomable no-man's lands, and I remained terrified at its threshold. Perhaps precisely because of my shyness, I soon became the pet of all the night workers who lived there. There was not a night in which a boisterous assembly of very lively courtesans did not gather around the reception table to tell stories until the early hours of the morning, but not before having brought me at least half a roasted chicken, accompanied by its corresponding Pepsi-Cola. It's also true that I made my own contributions: going on errands to buy them cigarettes, helping one of the women every time she had an epileptic attack, listening to their confidences, and so on.

The situation did not last. It wasn't long before the son of the Italian owner of the place, a long-haired guy who played guitar and pretended to be a hippie, asked me to quit my job. It did not help that, on several occasions, I had surreptitiously invited several acquaintances of mine without a fixed address to spend the night in one of the hotel rooms. One of them that I still remember vividly was named Pedro Zubr, a rather unsociable Polish "painter" who hung out in the cafés of Sabana Grande, often carrying one of his creations under his arm to see if anyone would buy it. I can still hear Pedro's scream the morning after sleeping at the hotel when, while he was showering, the water suddenly went from lukewarm to boiling without him having done anything.

One of my favorite stories from my time in the Hotel Capri is about Henri Charrière, owner of the Mi Vaca y Yo nightclub, the famous Papillon, who arrived in Venezuela after having escaped from the fearsome Devil's Island. There is a film from the 1970s about him, starring Steve McQueen in the role of Papillon, where his escape from the prison hell run by the French authorities on a Caribbean island near the coast of Venezuela is narrated.[23] According to Gladys, a very elegant and sophisticated woman who lived in the hotel and used its rooms for her nightly business, Charrière or Papillon more than once disappeared into one of those rooms with her and two other women, to enjoy the "show" that the three occasionally put together for the entertainment of one or another select client.

The final episode that closed my period in Sabana Grande was the ten days I spent with Jorge, an Argentine friend of the time, occupying the presidential suite of the Tamanaco Hotel. I had recently met Jorge and his other two Argentine friends, Eduardo and Cristina, in the Sabana Grande area. At that time, the three were passing through Caracas on their way to the United States, the promised land at the end of their tour of Latin America. My knowledge of much of the gastronomy of Francisco Solano at that time dates back to my meeting with those three travelers. From time to time, dressed in our best clothes, the three of us would sit down in one of the area's main restaurants to enjoy a copious lunch accompanied by the best wines. At the end of the meal, we asked to speak to the manager of the establishment, to inform him that we had no way to pay the bill. That must have happened three or four times, at least, and without exception they let us leave after making us sign a few receipts. It is not incidental that those were years of oil abundance. The fact is that it would not be long before Eduardo told us about his time at the Hilton Hotel in Caracas and the unpaid account he left there. As some say, the rest is history. After hearing Eduardo's story, it didn't take much for Jorge to convince me that we should spend a few days not at the Hilton—Eduardo's visit to that place was too recent for us to try anything in that respect—but at El Tamanaco, where we enjoyed ourselves for a while and took advantage of the benefits of that most luxurious Caracas hotel.

At that time, I had no fixed address and I slept in friends' cars and on their sofas. It is not surprising, then, that the prospect of spending a few days enjoying the many comforts of the most opulent hotel in Caracas acquired in my eyes the glow of utopia. A few days later, Jorge and I found ourselves at the foot of the main steps of the hotel with Jorge urging a couple of bellboys to hurry up with the suitcases. "Hurry up, Che, what an idiot you are!" That's how he rebuked them at the foot of the hotel steps, as I recall. Meanwhile, the two bellhops were busy loading the five or six suitcases that some friends had lent us a few days before, each one packed with heavy bricks. The idea, as I remember, was to enter the hotel in style. And something that Jorge definitely did not lack was a developed dramaturgical sense. During the days before our arrival at Tamanaco, he had convinced me to wear a blue blazer, provided by some friend or other, slick my hair, dividing it into two halves, and change my name from Rafael Sánchez to Rafael Ramallo Rosenthal, because, according to him, a Jewish surname always radiates money. I suppose that some anti-Semitic prejudice of his Buenos Aires roots must have played a role in his recommendation to add Rosenthal as my second surname. I remember having experienced some skepticism toward the proposal, which, however, I accepted because, as I saw things, Jorge's was the voice of experience. So, it was best not to ask too many questions. In those days credit cards did not yet exist, so, after checking into the hotel, the only thing we needed to do to enjoy the abundant dinners and other amenities of the establishment was to continue signing to our rooms. What followed was a series of pool parties and lavish banquets, a couple of times attended by our friends. The only time in my life that I have tasted frogs' legs occurred during that stay at El Tamanaco. These festivities were, needless to say, always presided over by the omnipresent fear of being discovered.

Every time we needed to move around Caracas, we had to leave the hotel on foot along the beautiful slope that connects the Tamanaco with Las Mercedes and, once below, start to hitchhike. My main concern throughout the journey was to not raise my feet too high when walking, so that the holes in the sole of each shoe would not be visible from behind. Things ended as they had to end, with us detained at the fearsome Catia jail, waiting for my father to pay the exorbitant hotel bill. How could it be otherwise, given that we (my friends and I) had not a bolivar [penny] in our pockets?

Just after arriving at the jail, when Jorge and I were standing in a long line of detainees waiting for our personal data to be processed so we could be detained, one of the officials ordered us to all strip down to our underwear. What horror did I not feel when Jorge emerged from his jeans wearing pink boxers printed with bright green polka dots? "Hey, I want that blondie!" That was the least of the remarks shouted between whistles and jokes to my Argentine companion. After that introduction, the following days in the cell (a mere four-by-two-meter room with a toilet in the middle, as I recall), which we occupied with twelve or fourteen other detainees, were spent with Jorge singing tangos, one after another without stopping, as enormous tears rolled down his cheeks.

Clearly, "The Cat," "The Terror of the Pharmacies," "The Little Monkey," and our other ten or twelve cellmates were determined lovers of the genre. Hence, no matter how hoarse he became, it was enough for Jorge to finish singing a tango that they would urge him to start with the next one. And so, tango after tango, my poor friend was losing his voice. Given the circumstances, it is not surprising that the jail authorities managed to soften me up. After just three or four days in jail, and having met two or three times with the authorities, I not only confessed to them my real name, but I also provided them with my family's address and telephone number. My father ultimately paid the outstanding bills. Thank goodness, since, otherwise, the least that would have happened to me would have been to emerge from the mishap with a police record. In fact, the police authorities had kept us in the jail without even taking our fingerprints, all probably in the hope of using the threat of a formal booking as leverage to extract payment. That's how things were in those days in Venezuela (let's not even talk about the present!). As for Jorge, who, with his Buenos Aires accent, the authorities surely never identified as a good candidate to settle the account, the last I heard from him was in a postcard he sent me from Los Angeles, where he ended up residing. He told me how much fun he was having there. Praising the "comforts" of the American lifestyle, he told me that he spent the whole day lying down watching television with his hands crossed behind his head in a deliciously chilled environment. The good life.

Broadly speaking, what followed was an overland tour through several South American countries, accompanied by a Chilean girlfriend. The final destination was Allende's Chile, which I soon had to leave through the Venezuelan embassy, at which I sought refuge with Gilberto, a very close Venezuelan friend, a few days after the coup d'état against the leftist regime on September 11, 1973. I still have the edition of *El Universal* where, to my eternal shame, I appear in a photo on the front page, half covering my face with a newspaper while, along with other repatriates, I descend the steps of one of the planes that the Venezuelan government had sent to Chile to pick up Venezuelan refugees at the embassy. I covered my face in the naive hope that my parents wouldn't recognize me. Until that moment, both of my parents believed that I had stayed on in Quito, to which I had been sent after being denied entry into Chile. I had managed to return.

At that time, I did not have a Venezuelan passport and was frequently stopped at international borders and temporarily incarcerated. When I had attempted to enter Chile, Fidel Castro was on a state visit, and my Cuban birth made me appear to be a possible threat. Hence my initial deportation to Peru. When the dictatorship came to power in Chile, in September 1973, my father wrote to me in the hope that—finally!—the new "climate of peace and tranquility" of the dictatorship might also surround my studies, enveloping the whole region. The letter arrived with my Chilean girlfriend—or, as she was called then, "compañera"—at the embassy where I had sought refuge along with another Venezuelan friend. The story of how my father finally found out that I was in Allende's Chile and not in Quito—as I had made him believe so that he would continue sending me the modest allowance of fifty dollars a month that until then he had provided—is too convoluted to tell here. But I was later told that the resounding, "*¡Coño, Carajo!*" (roughly,

"Fuck, Damned!") pronounced by my father from one of the seats in a darkened movie theater when he saw me on a newsreel, coming down the steps of the military plane, was epic. After that, I didn't hear from my family again for about two or three years.

What happened in Chile was traumatic enough for me to, once and for all, put aside my worst fears about how my family would react if they found out that I was involved in leftist activities. Shortly after returning from Chile, without thinking too much about it, I made the decision, first, to do political work in the neighborhoods of the Catia area, and, eventually, to join the MIR (Movement of the Revolutionary Left) of Caracas where I had a relatively brief internship with my friend Máximo. I must confess that, ultimately, political militancy was not for me. I remember the approximately three years that I spent as an activist as a horribly endless, not to say boring, string of meetings with neighborhood groups, bringing to them at each meeting, with only minimal variation, the same, unbearably tedious "party line." At that time, I was ostensibly working as a research assistant at CONICIT (National Council for Scientific and Technological Research), driving a rather dilapidated Volkswagen Beetle and studying in fits and starts at the Universidad Central de Venezuela (UCV) School of Sociology. As for how I managed to reconcile my work as a militant with maintaining a regular job, let's say that one of the ways of doing so was a note that read, "Gone for coffee, I'll be right back," that I periodically left on my desk. I often showed up at the institution about a fortnight after leaving that or another similar note, usually to pick up my biweekly check and to chat with friends. Beyond the generosity of my supervisor, whose name I withhold and who was aware of my political adventures, it occurs to me that my job stability at that time, and the fact that I was never fired from CONICIT, had a lot to do with the character of the so-called Saudi Venezuela of the 1970s.

Then came a first marriage, and then a journey, first, to California, to take a degree in anthropology, and then, after a brief stay in Caracas, to Chicago, in 1981. By then, I was already thirty-one years old, and my trip to the Windy City of the North American Midwest had the objective of pursuing a doctorate in anthropology at the University of Chicago. There, to my great fortune, I met Patricia Spyer, my current wife, whom I adore, and who has made me a better person than I would undoubtedly have been if she had not been by my side. At the time we met, we were both first-year students in the anthropology program at that university. And with my arrival in Chicago, my life of adventures finally came to an end. Although, fortunately, anthropology has its wonderful islands of time outside of time called fieldwork, at least seen from the outside, my existence from then on, to a certain extent, adapted itself to the rhythms of the everyday life of a peaceful "scholar." That is, seen from the outside. "Interior" upheaval is another matter.

I could continue indefinitely narrating the incidents of my life before my departure to the United States to study anthropology. However, for my purposes here, I think what has been said is enough. I prefer to follow the reverse route now, and, instead of proceeding in an approximately chronological order, as I have done to this point, to pick up the thread following the opposite trajectory. Or, in words that some attribute to the *Benemérito* Juan Vicente Gómez, to tell what I still have to tell "from present to the past." My retrospective journey begins in the mountains of Sorte, in the state of Yaracuy, more precisely in Quibayo, on a sunny morning in 1994, where I am doing fieldwork with a view to obtaining my doctorate in anthropology.

Someone lies horizontally on the ground inside a circle of brightly lit candles: around him, a fairly large group of people, of which I am a part, chant the same refrain over and over again:

"Give him, him, give him *force*! [*fuerza*]."[24]

"Give him force!"

Meanwhile, as if shaken by an electric current, the recumbent figure is overcome by a succession of sudden spasms. The relationship between the calls for force and the spasms that attack that figure seem causal, as if the calls for strength immediately translate into the spasmodic behavior of the patient. From time to time, uttering a series of unintelligible grunts, someone with a red scarf tied around his head staggers over to the recumbent to blow a puff of tobacco smoke into his face; or, if not, he stops to pour a mouthful of brandy in his face after having theatrically taken a swig from the bottle that he always holds by the neck with his left hand, more or less at the height of his thigh.

A beating of drums accompanies the scene, redundantly confirming, modulating, and amplifying in another register the requests for strength made by those gathered. To one side, arranged at the foot of a tree just behind the group of drummers, is an improvised altar piled with multicolored plaster figurines illuminated, from time to time, by a series of candles. The complex is presided over by the plaster bust of a female figure flanked, on one side, by the bust, also in plaster, of an Indigenous chief; on the other, by that of a Black soldier dressed in the characteristic Napoleonic uniform of patriotic officers from the time of independence. Oddly, the central female figure reminds me of Snow White. The busts of the three figures emerge from the same elongated pedestal that joins them together from the chest upward, as part of an indissoluble whole, made of colored plaster. Everything takes place in a supremely idyllic setting. Suffused with a rather strong smell of incense, alcohol, and other less recognizable substances, the scene is bathed in sunlight that filters in from high above the heads of the participants through the crowns of towering trees. Depending on which way the wind is blowing, a faint smell of excrement occasionally wafts through the air.

Many Venezuelan readers, especially if they are anthropologists, and some non-Venezuelans, will have no difficulty recognizing in what I have just described a possession scene from the cult of María Lionza. Present in the three plaster figurines presiding over the altar are the "Three Powers" or the three spiritual powers "of highest light" of the cult as a whole: Queen María Lionza, Negro Primero, and Cacique Guaicaipuro. What is at stake is that the recumbent figure incorporates one or another of the spirits associated with the cult. Now, as I recount this scene, the resonance between it and that other, many years ago, on the sunny terrace of my family's apartment in Madrid, shortly after I received my father's slap, becomes inescapable to me. To begin with, in both scenes the central figure lying on the ground is overcome by strong spasms: in the one in Madrid, mine; in the space of María Lionza, that of the cult member. In both scenes, force plays a clearly leading role, in the sense that the spasms that afflict the recumbent figure in each of them are nothing more than reverberations of that force, at once exterior and invasive. So much so, that the situation of each figure is unintelligible apart from the field of forces that acts on each. So much for the similarities.

The differences between the scenes are no less notable. They have to do, first, with the way the vectors of force behave in each one, vertically in the Madrid scene, horizontally in María Lionza's. If not physically since, at the time, my father was not much taller than me, at least symbolically, force in the Madrid scene acts from top to bottom. It is vertical, unleashed by the resounding slap that the Father gives his son in the living room of the family apartment.

Something very different takes place in María Lionza's scene. There the force acts not vertically but horizontally. In accordance with beliefs entertained by the cultists, and attracted by their requests, in this scene the force enters the horizontal figure through the feet after he has crawled like a snake along the ground. And not only that. In principle, the requests for strength ("give him force/strength") are addressed in the plural to the invisible assembly of spirits that hovers over the cultists at all times. The goal of these requests is to move the spirits to send one of their number to possess the prostrated figure, thereby imbuing it with their strength. In this interpretation, the ultimate origin of the force that ends up possessing the cult member, eventually raising it from the ground, is none other than the invisible mass of the dead to which Canetti alludes in his book *Crowds and Power*. In that sense, the singular spirit that ends up taking possession of the recumbent figure is clearly a detachment from that numinous constellation that, at all times, hovers over the cultists.

Less literally, it is also possible to say that this force flows horizontally from the cultists' requests toward the recumbent figure around which the others are gathered. In that sense, these requests would be, in their own right, a means by which the community of cultists imparts to one of its members the strength that is disseminated among all of them—and this on a horizontal axis. Although ostensibly directed to the spirits, these requests are, in themselves, very powerful vectors of force; they crystallize good wishes, affection, longings for the future, desires for protection and care, and, in general, the broad emotional spectrum that is always at play whenever someone asks for strength, either for themselves or for others.

Closely related to the preceding observation, a second difference between the two scenes concerns the fate that awaits the figure at the center of each. Thus, in the Madrid scene, knocked to the ground by the paternal slap, like the beetle at the end of Kafka's story, the prostrated figure is destined to be obliterated, finally swept away by a broom during cleaning.[25] The same cannot be said of what happens in the possession scene of María Lionza. Far from being destined for destruction, everything that happens in this latter scene suggests that the forces operating within it seek not to knock down but to lift the recumbent body of the cultist from the ground so that it can act as a medium or matter for one or another spirit. The aim is for the spirit to use this material to alleviate the sufferings, shortcomings, and aspirations, both spiritual and material, of those who come to request its services. What is at stake in this scene is to prepare the bodily matter so that, once its own spirit has momentarily abandoned it, it can receive one or another of the many spirits associated with the cult, whether that of an Indigenous chief, the doctor José Gregorio Hernández, a Viking warrior, a Hindu love goddess, an Egyptian pharaoh, President Nixon, or, to name one more among the many other possibilities, an actor from the golden age of Mexican cinema.

The last difference I would like to highlight concerns the emotional temperature inherent in the forces unleashed in each of the two scenes. Thus, in the Madrid scene the paternal slap exclusively communicates rage. In its intention to petrify its victim, this paternal anger scares away from the scene any other emotion capable of laterally removing it away from or beyond the condition of abjection to which it has been reduced. Once again, exercised from top down by both the state and the family, the terror instantiated in the Madrid scene seeks to isolate that victim from any surrounding affectivity in order to constitute him as a self-contained being, subject to authority. The emotional climate in María Lionza's possession scene is considerably more complex;

unlike what I experienced with my father in Madrid, it can in no way be reduced to one dominant emotion exclusive of all others. Even if the spirit being propitiated is that of a Viking or an Indigenous chieftain, the affectivity of that spirit is not reducible to a single emotion, such as ferocity or warlike rage. From the beginning, this affectivity positions that spirit in an interwoven network of relationships with the affections, interests, expectations, and desires of all those who at that moment request its spiritual help. The bodily matter that finally rises from the ground possessed by one spirit or another does so to insert itself into the emotional and affective world of all those gathered around it and who until that moment have been imbuing it with their affections and emotions, looking to raise it from its prostration.

This affective universe positions matter in a network of relationships saturated with affectivity that precede it and from which the most intimate being of each cultist ultimately emerges. Rather than being given a priori, the cult makes explicit through its practices and its invocations how much each person's being is an eminently porous entity that mutates incessantly as the constellation of forces, emotions, and identities that it encounters outside itself shapes its interior. Not for a moment does the cult fail to underline the centrality of the body or matter of the cultists as an obligatory theater where the forces that constantly act on it are modulated and channeled. One of the central objectives of the cult's practices and invocations is, precisely, to strengthen this matter by lifting it from the ground where the blows of an intractable destiny formed by state violence, a lack of love, poor health, or unemployment have rendered it painfully prostrate. This in order to empower that being so that, without restrictions of the kind generally induced from above, by the established powers, it can mimetically incorporate one or another spirit that, due to the spirit's personality and emotional disposition, is most capable of dealing with the form of affliction suffered by whoever approaches the cult in search of relief.

It is important to note that the body or matter of the cultist is not passive. The ability of matter to receive spirits is not something that occurs spontaneously from one moment to the next. Any member of the cult who exhibits a predisposition to being possessed by spirits must undergo a fairly lengthy apprenticeship. That cultist, in other words, must "learn" to be matter. To do this, she or he must undergo an elaborate series of practices and procedures orchestrated by those mediums and their assistants in charge of the "portal" that she or he has chosen as the most suitable place to learn to receive spirits. One exemplary act or moment in this process is called *ramalazo*, and occurs when a would-be medium is struck with a branch, whose many smaller boughs and offshoots may be read as symbols of the multiplicity to which the apprentice's matter is to become receptive. "Portal" is the term that the followers of María Lionza use to designate any space of devotion organized in a cult member's family home. It must be facilitated by at least one medium, and his or her assistants, who are referred to as "banks," in a sense that implies both support and the storage of energy. The purpose of this apprenticeship is to learn how the body or matter of the neophyte can become a theater capable of staging and modulating the material and spiritual forces that strive to possess it without, at the same time, being overwhelmed and devastated by them. This is precisely to prevent the catastrophes like the one I suffered at the house of my father's friend in Miami Beach, so many years ago. If learning to be matter presupposes a relatively prolonged educational process, this is by no means accidental. It is only when this learning has been completed that the matter is finally enabled to receive the spirits, its body fortified so that they can speak and act through it. In the absence of this learning, the subjects simply decompose, as happened to me at the house in Miami Beach. Overtaken in their corporeality by an unmanageable exterior, these subjects are summarily pushed aside by the alterity that they do not know how to channel and that, like so many other broken toys, leaves them floating adrift.

This detour through the learning process of the cultists is intended to suggest that, more than a starting point, María Lionza's scene is a point of arrival where, with the essential emotional and affective support of the audience, the subject is raised from the ground by spirits. What I want to highlight here is the fundamental role that, from the beginning, and not only in the scene described, the audience's affectivity plays in this process. For the subject candidate to finally be possessed by the spirits, one condition must be met without exception: from the beginning, those in charge of its formation must have been lovingly there to receive it. Without the apprentice's willingness to trust in the love of that audience, in the conviction that his patrons in the "spiritual realm" wish him well, the material candidate will in no way successfully venture into the dark night of possession. Without the trust generated in this process—the firm belief that, like the net of the trapeze artist, your sponsors are there to bring you ashore in any eventuality—the learning process simply would not come to fruition. Nothing less than that blind faith is necessary to assume the vulnerability required to deliver oneself to such alterity.

From beginning to end, the achievement of possession depends on the ability of the cult practices to insert the candidate as matter into a territory traversed by powerful affective, emotional, and spiritual currents. In that territory nothing and no one, neither the mediums or the subjects, nor their banks or assistants, nor the apprentices, nor the clients, are at any time identical to what they were before participating in the cult. They all continually become what they are through their participation in this universe densely saturated with emotion. In this sense, the process of preparing the subjects consists of channeling and modulating the currents that at all times circulate among its members, to put them at the service of an already decided objective. For the rest, impregnated with affectivity and interwoven by encounters and exchanges in the most heterogeneous situations, in that territory or no-man's-land where "matters" routinely offer themselves as transitory abodes for spirits, blending more or less fleetingly with them, agency and vulnerability are not opposed to each other, but rather presuppose each other. Something that is always the case, but that the cult of María Lionza powerfully highlights, is how much, far from preceding the world, agency and identity are always inhabited, better yet, possessed by the alterity that constitutes them from within.

All of this resonates with my observations about Plaza Altamira. It also resonates with what my encounter with 1960s Venezuela and its tumultuous democratic sociability meant to me after the years spent first in Batista's Cuba, and, later, in Franco's Spain. To limit myself to Plaza Altamira: if there is a common denominator between the plaza of the few short months in my adolescence and the pilgrimage centers of María Lionza, it is the fact that, at least to a certain extent, in both places the constitution and reconstitution of subjects was a relatively open process, contingent upon continually changing and relatively unpredictable circumstances and configurations. Unlike Franco's Spain, where the vertical constitution of subjects as monads isolated through fear prevailed, the situation was different in both Plaza Altamira and the María Lionza cult. Despite the thirty years that passed between the two experiences, and despite how much

Venezuela changed during those years, something that both the Plaza and the mountains of Sorte had in common was a tumultuous, extraordinarily rich, and relatively unpredictable sociability.

Nothing could be further from the emotional misery of Francoism, where a good part of the regime's energies was directed toward preventing horizontal contagion among people in order to better constitute them as isolated subjects solely answerable to power (of the state, of the school, of the family), than the contagious, intrinsically democratic sociability typical of both the Plaza Altamira of my adolescence and the María Lionza cult of my first fieldwork. To these two arenas I would have to add at least the Plaza Venezuela that welcomed me upon my arrival in Venezuela, the Sabana Grande of my adolescence, and the bustling evenings until late at night in the prostitutes' hotel in that same area, or, more recently, and also in Sabana Grande, the space of evangelical Thomist squatters among whom I did my last fieldwork. In constitutive tension with the vertical power of the state, all of them were the scene of a tumultuous mass sociability that could not be further from what was the norm under Franco. To the contrary, all these areas were the scene of an incessant emotional contagion where, unlike what happened during Franco's Spain, nothing remained identical to itself—not for a moment. With all that this implies of an uninterrupted mimetic adoption of new identities and modes of conduct, not identity but the ethos of Rimbaud's "I am an other" was what ultimately predominated there.

If what is at stake is apprehending what distinguished Franco's Spain from the democratic Venezuela that welcomed me upon my arrival in Caracas in the mid-1960s, then there is nothing better than paying attention to the radically opposed ways in which the urban masses occupied public spaces in those two places. Thus, while in Franco's

Spain the presence of the masses in public spaces tended to be entirely orchestrated by the state, in Venezuela things happened differently. From the time of my arrival in the country in the early sixties, that massive presence insinuated itself in me with the force of an original sociality that democratically overflowed all the institutional frameworks designed to shape and contain it.

Traversed by the "general problematic of mimesis" (Lacoue-Labarthe and Nancy[26]), what, following these authors, I call "The Mother" is precisely the domain of a primal sociality like the one I have just alluded to, where, beyond established identities, what predominates is the incessant alteration of each and every one of them. "The Mother," which as a term must be distinguished from actual mothers, indicates a form of affectivity and productivity that is not dictated by prohibition. Excessive with respect to any totalization of life from above, whether by the state or any other institutionalized agency, and frequently overlooked, that sociality is the relatively inapprehensible maternal substance that suffuses the whole social field. Institutional forms nevertheless continually try to apprehend, shape, and govern it. Interwoven with emotions, identities, and multiple affectivities, if some in Venezuela call this excessive territory "matriarchal," and associate it with the cult of María Lionza, it is due to that same complexity and affective multiplicity that in many places is associated with the maternal figure. It can well be said that in that no-man's-land, the emotional one-sidedness of the Father is suspended and replaced by the enveloping emotional complexity of "The Mother," an accumulation of emotions that are often conflicting and not necessarily benevolent (but sometimes enabling mutual aid), and that are full of both possibilities and threats. Continuously overflowing the vertical economies of the patriarchal regime, no one is identical to themselves in the unfathomable regions of "La Madre." Drawn horizontally by the powerful emotional currents that continually circulate there and to which, fatally, we are all exposed, in those territories we all continually become others. As in the endless stories that my mother told me in her best moments, there even the most terrifying parents can become restless dwarfs moving hurriedly through the labyrinthine tunnels of some mine in distant South Africa.

By baptizing this substratum with the name of a female figure—who, more accurately, is the Mother of God herself, the Virgin Mary—Venezuelans are not misguided. In a country where the heroic state that arose with independence has for more than two hundred years done little more than heroically brutalize the people, to the point that the country has been reduced to a chaos of smoking ruins, calling that which elsewhere remains unnameable "María Lionza" is, among other things, to recognize the crucial role that this figure plays in the continual constitution and continued reconstitution of the network of exchanges, benefits, and affections inherent to that original sociality. It is thanks to this maternal excess that the country somehow manages to resist the relentless onslaught of the local Leviathan. Far from being the obstacle to modernity that some claim, if we are not yet the dust to which the heroic state and its supposed modernities have always promised to consign us, this is due to the protection that, for better or worse, "The Mother" still offers. Slightly modifying what the poet San Juan de la Cruz wrote regarding the transcendence of love, "We will be dust, but an enamored dust!" (¡*Polvo seremos, más polvo enamorado!*).

When we allow ourselves to be guided by some cultist and enter into the maternal territories of María Lionza, it can well be said that we have left behind the domain of the Father and his rigidly prescribed identities to venture into the unfathomable regions of the Mother. Indulging in a truly dizzying game, as if it were an everyday occurrence, the subjects of María Lionza's cult mimetically adopt, one after another, a potentially infinite series of masks. Depending on what the circumstances require—getting a job, healing from an illness, resolving a matter with the law or finding a lover, or, more Hamlet-like, deflecting the darts of merciless fortune—these subjects choose the most appropriate apparition for their objective from the many possible identities from which they can always choose. Using for these purposes the vast repertoire of identities that the cult makes available, in these maternal domains anyone can mimetically become anything, from a miraculous doctor, a goddess of Hindu love, or a singer from the golden age of cinema. From Mexican to Malandro Freddy, India Rosa, the Father of the Nation Simón Bolívar, to the Indigenous chief Guaicaipuro. Blowing his horn in the early hours of the morning, encouraging his companions to raid some sleepy Saxon chicken-keeping village, Viking Eric the Red is also in this local pantheon. On one occasion when I was visiting Sorte, an Egyptian pharaoh surrounded by his entire court of followers even made an appearance in those domains! All of this is tantamount to saying that it is not identity but identification that prevails in the numinous domains of the Queen.

The extraordinary thing about a cult like that of María Lionza is that, in a powerfully synthetic way, it brings together in one place all the versatility, porosity, mimicry, and tendency to change forms that, perhaps in a more diffuse way but not necessarily less effectively, occurs in the varied scenarios inherent to Venezuelan sociality as a whole: from government offices, markets, and public squares to the churches and evangelical congregations where, today, a good part of the social and political life of the country takes place. Since it is generally necessary to respond as flexibly as possible to ambiguity-saturated and highly fluid situations, any pretense at consistency has to take a backseat. On such slippery terrain, what really counts is adapting to whatever comes, mimetically adopting the identities and behaviors that best correspond to the changing landscape in which one must move. When injustice, inequality, poor health, heartbreak, or unemployment lurks around every corner, remaining in the place that power assigns and remaining identical to oneself is equivalent to becoming a target for every misfortune. Or, what is the same: if you behave according to the dictates that come from above and exhibit the behavior and identities requested by those in power, then you become paralyzed, deprived of any ability to respond to the deluge that falls upon you when you least expect it. Instead, you wait for it to come upon you, exhibit the flexibility necessary to adopt the identities required to navigate the changing circumstances in which you continually find yourself immersed. Then, maybe, you have a chance. As the main character of a popular Venezuelan soap opera in the nineties used to say, "As we go, we see what to do" (*Según vamos yendo, vamos viendo*).

Far from some character flaw of the Venezuelan people, whose intelligence should be "revolutionized," as some would say (the *Revolution of Intelligence* is the title of a singularly pernicious little book that appeared in Venezuela toward the end of the seventies, mentioned previously), the porosity and plasticity that Venezuelans exhibit in heterogeneous circumstances is in fact linked to survival itself. One thing that María Lionza powerfully reveals is the degree to which individuals must nimbly set aside hegemonic identities, and opportunistically adopt the ones that become available, simply to survive in a place like Venezuela. In many ways, the Venezuelan state continues to operate along the lines of sovereignty as described by Michel Foucault, where the state seeks to unload the full weight of its sovereignty on subjects every time it catches them red-handed, despite the ambitions expressed by some intellectuals for a regime of discipline and less despotic punishment. In this context, anyone who fails to embrace a mimetically self-transforming orientation courts condemnation. Among other powerful reasons, this is why, as in María Lionza's cult, one can in principle be anything in Venezuela. If one adds to this the fact that the characters who routinely possess cult mediums come overwhelmingly from the mass media, and especially from television, then the image of Venezuelan sociability as a space devoid of borders and fixed identities—where the here and there, the real and the virtual continually exchange places—begins to take shape. In that intensely media-saturated milieu, any pretense at possessing an identity that remains unchanged despite changing circumstances is continually subverted by the power of those circumstances to shape each and every one of those identities. Rosalind Morris's dazzling essay[27] on the relationships between presence and exposure to alterity in the practice of possession, as mediated by media technology, offers an exceptional avenue for apprehending how, along with other factors, these technologies modulate and contribute to the specific texture of socialities such as the Venezuelan one.

Caused by the profound crisis of representation (political, economic, religious) that has afflicted Venezuela since approximately the mid-eighties, the most varied scenarios throughout the country have been filled with a proliferating mass sociality that continually overflows the institutional frameworks designed to shape and contain it. The fact that for a few years now this sociality has been dominating public squares, occupied buildings, informal markets, and every other place where strangers meet more or less at random, without being protected by established institutions, cannot but have profound consequences. In all these areas it is as if "The Mother" had returned to reclaim from "The Father" her domain, which for a time had been precariously governed and articulated by patriarchal economies. Precariously, because in more obvious and explicit ways than in other places, and for reasons that have to do with the overwhelming founding violence of the wars of independence some two hundred years ago, and that I explore in my book *Dancing Jacobins*, in Venezuela any control that the patriarchal state may have over the forms of daily life is in continuous tension with The Mother, who fatally destabilizes it from within. As I have already suggested, the fact that in Venezuela this primordial sociality has its own name and is called María Lionza is already a measure of how much, in Venezuela (relative to other places), that formless and flexible "being-together" not only does not completely elude consciousness, or escape the behavior and expectations of Venezuelans, but provides the environment in which these may develop. Taking place on the margins of, or even extrinsic to social movements, churches, unions, political parties, and to a large extent, unformed by and excessive with respect to these institutional structures, the scenarios of that sociality are also the scope of an incessant mimesis that transforms them into very powerful instigators of social, political, aesthetic, and personal change. For the mass sociality that concerns me in these writings, the future is not teleologically conceived. In all its disruptive force and potential, the future is always arriving.

The Three Squares: Being, Having Been, Being Another

by Luis Pérez-Oramas

In the enlightening text entrusted to us by Rafael Sánchez, an anthropologist of the Venezuelan polis if there ever has been one, the writer seems to counter the famous ontological path summarized in Aristotle's dictum: the what it was to be—*to ti en einai*. Louis Marin used to begin his classes on the autobiographical power of representation, often thinking of his much-admired Stendhal, by recalling the Stagirite's dialogue with the old Solon to show his students that the narration of autobiography is, par excellence, the impossible story. It is possible that to be is what it was to be, my teacher seemed to say, but the two foundational phrases of the story that can be narrated as autobiography are literally unpronounceable: "I was born," "I died." By force majeure and inexorably, both of these statements escape the realm of experience and both resist becoming memory.

The reader holds in their hands a speculative, political testament, dressed as an autobiographical narrative. It is the story of one of the last great men of the Republic. Knowing that the dismantling of the heroic patriarchy that constitutes the authoritarian root of the (failed) state in Venezuela has been Sánchez's permanent vocation, I nonetheless want to maintain the appellation—great man—for Sánchez, an intellectual bent on reclaiming the Maternity of the nation, the collective Mother that is the tumultuous sociability of the Venezuelan country. The great men of the Republic, *viri heroici sublimis*, but one must not forget the great women (*dominae heroici sublimis*), include Luisa Cáceres, Fermín Toro, Mariano Picón, Mercedes Fermin, Sofia Imber, Maria Teresa Otero, Luis Castro Leiva, Rafael Cadenas, and now, in addition, Rafael Sánchez—among others. In some cases, we will have to reflect, ethically, on the shortcuts of fortune that have made the vastness of their works coincide with the brevity of life.

Contrary to Aristotle's account, this political testament, written in the painful experience of a particular end time, tells us that to be is to be another, to be able to be another, to be becoming another. Against the violent hardness of hierarchical and patriarchal imposition, against the brutal swipe of the (failed) state, only too ready to catch us red-handed, the spasmodic possibility of alterity is for Venezuelans a salvation more than an escape route: a resounding answer. And Sánchez invites us to understand that in this permanent breach of multiple alterity, in its nooks and crannies—perhaps dark—lies the possibility for Venezuelans to "in principle be anything."

Obviously, the "tumultuous democratic sociability" of the Venezuelan people cannot be, nor be understood as, an essence. In this set of "acknowledgments" (*reconocimientos*), Rafael Sánchez invites us to understand that the claim of identification (against identity) contains the historicity of our own tumultuous and dancing condition. Perhaps the foundational stone (or one of them) of such an understanding is his own landmark book: *Dancing Jacobins: A Venezue-*

lan Genealogy of Latin American Populism.[1] There, between the spasmodic body that dances and the hierarchical monumentality of the marble hero, our redundant tendency to construct plastered leaderships, incapable of accounting for, nor truly belonging to the social body of which they are the dominant outgrowth, is described.

Against those "fathers" of the homeland, Rafael Sánchez erects the salutary figure of an amorphous, dynamic, metamorphic, tempestuous, feverish, jovial, festive, unceasingly changing maternity in face and voice, embodying the people against the State. He quotes Pierre Clastres, who lived among Venezuelans of the Yanomami ethnicity, discovering the real, historical condition of possibility of a power-without-power, of a society without a dominant and centralizing power.[2] And he focuses, above all, on the place of that unpredictable, sentimental, emotive, and at times orgiastic matria that usually appears in the public square.

Autobiographical, Sánchez's text skillfully escapes the pitfalls of the impossible narrative. It is a collection of memories and already exists, fully, in the heart of the remembered. It begins, curiously, with a baptismal scene: not the baptism of Christians, but rather that of a paternal anointment — or rather punishment — of the body with cold water. But what stands out, what is celebrated, what coincides with the open field of freedom in this text are the places of arrival — not the departures, nor the origin. It is the future that is becoming in the form of a populous square, and via a riotous appropriation of spaces that belong to everyone. Here, "everyone" names the incessant transformation of everyone.

Rafael Sánchez was born in Batista's Cuba and grew up in Franco's Spain. Arriving in Venezuela permitted him to reach a place where all imperative verticality breaks down. There are three moving phrases that punctuate the end of this essay-story, this fable of life from where a possible theory of everyone emerges: "Venezuela was for me freedom," "Venezuela was for me the multitude," "Venezuela was for me democracy." Each of these statements is summarized in another, at once more intimate and perhaps more powerful statement: "Venezuela was for me friendship." That phrase echoes an intellectual attempt that Sánchez is aware of, and that Jacques Derrida at the end of his life proposed as a dismantling of the genealogical and phallocentric primacy of civic virtue as patriarchal virility.[3] It suggests the convocation—even if only nominal—of a politics of friendship.

The places of friendship are multiform. The places of friendship are polymorphic. The places of friendship are protean. Every friendship is a square that opens up, defined between two or more lives. And in Sánchez's text, the squares also form a trilogy: Plaza Venezuela opening up suddenly as a possible landscape, endless, to the adolescent who has just arrived; Plaza Altamira as a place of encounters where the author's memory condenses unforgettable images of police running like swarms behind prostitutes, who move like avian flocks in the ephemeral sky of happiness. Finally, the swampy, drunken, spasmodic square of metamorphosis in the rituals of Sorte, next to the matronymic gentilic of María Lionza.

Because Venezuela reaches Rafael Sánchez in the square that bears the name of the nation, and then in the hills of Sorte, I will allow myself a brief digression about the accidental centrality of the urban topology of Caracas. It has been a long time since the equestrian statue of the monumental hero—Bolívar—has ceased marking the center of the city. The first strategic displacements of this centrality occurred in the nineteenth century, during Antonio Guzmán Blanco's regime. Then, engineers Jesús Muñoz Tebar and Juan Hurtado Manrique took down and carried off the old statuary to signal the expiry of the regime embodied by the Christian temple. Then they built the Masonic temple in an almost symmetrically opposed angle to the old church, from north to east. Indicating the future that the lettered positivism of the time wanted to materialize, they substituted for the old Christian Church—Santa Teresa—names from the saints' calendar that were similar to those of the caudillo Guzmán Blanco's wife, Ana and Teresa, located to the south and west of central Plaza Bolívar. A century later, the constitutive tensions of the republic continued to produce, perhaps by accident, more twists: the architect Carlos Raúl Villanueva grimly rejected the notion that the sculpture of María Lionza by Alejandro Colina could be in the cosmopolitan and modern Olympian enclosure of the university campus that he had designed, excluding it and placing it in the middle of the main highway that goes through the city. Then-president Rafael Caldera ordered the erection of the seated statue of Andrés Bello in nearby Plaza Venezuela, using an unprecedented iconography for a nation's founder that broke free from the model of the armed heroic horse rider. It is not hard to identify in both figures the object of exile: of vernacular and popular beliefs and cults (María Lionza) by the elite culture; of intelligence, logos, grammar (Bello) by the chieftainship of pure violence and epic voluntarism. As if it were the figure of a possible future or another utopia, the organic and labyrinthine body of the city itself, protean and uncontrollable, does not cease to grow in the narrow valley where Humboldt had not seen any capacity for more than a million inhabitants. And thus, inscribing by chance, residually, but incontrovertibly, both monuments—that of the exiled intellectual and that of the atavistic and maternal goddess—now serve as the true center of the capital, as the capital coordinate of the nation.[4]

Some time ago, a young artist came to me with a set of ambitious questions. Expecting a technical answer, he inquired about the contributions of modernity in the field of visual arts. I truly do not know if modernity invented any unprecedented form of image—the moving image, perhaps, but we all know that images do not move, or speak, except when we move them or make them speak in our own voice. That day it occurred to me to say that the only true invention of modernity was public space: not necessarily the square, or the place for the multitudes, coliseums, arenas, forums, or amphitheaters whose existence precedes the modern. But the conceptual instance of a place that cannot belong to anyone and that can only belong to everyone. Such is the place of both the republic and democracy.

The place where the people are, as José Bergamín clamored in the presence of Giorgio Agamben, a remnant, always remains of the people. This is the place to which we can never cease to aspire to be all, but in which we can never, not one, coincide with our own totality: the place where, in the end, populism might break down. Rafael Sánchez summons us to understand that place, to embody it, to come to be in its changes, to welcome there the future that does not cease to be coming. He asks us to consider the alterity through which Venezuelan sociability survives injustice and the monumental arbitrariness of the (failed) patriarchal and violent State. He urges us to reflect on how it gives itself to the festive dance without heroes where we are always others, where to be is what we are yet to be, what we might be.

Afterword
Claudio Lomnitz

The book published here as *Reconocimientos: A Memoir of Becoming* is a singular text where self-discovery opens up to anthropological discovery, while anthropology offers a key that allows the author to better understand his own experience.

I say that this is a unique essay because I can't identify a similar text to this curiously baroque and modern great-grandchild of Michel de Montaigne, in which critique and biography illuminate one another in a light that is at once loving and relentless. Throughout its brave pages, this account of the life of Rafael Sánchez—who is one of Latin America's most original anthropologists—delivers a true discovery concerning Venezuelan culture and sociability, and through it, Sánchez also uncovers a political dialectic that is manifest in various permutations throughout the Spanish-speaking Americas.

The way in which autobiographical reflection leads Sánchez to conceive of this dialectic is astonishing. Rafael was born in Cuba in the final years of Fulgencio Batista's long dictatorship, and he left the island as a child, ten years old, prompted by the Cuban Revolution. He was first sent alone to Miami. Later, his family joined him, and together they traveled to Franco's Spain. Those years are recounted with memorable precision in this book; they are a time of subjection to strict familial and societal authority. Rafael's arrival in Venezuela, on the other hand, offered him an unexpected opportunity: emancipation from his family. The libertarian country that offered Rafael Sánchez his freedom also provided, in time, the fertile ground in which Sánchez the anthropologist was born. In this regard at least, this memoir can be read as a *bildungsroman* of sorts, though of course it is an essay and not a novel: through its pages we witness the birth of a new subject, in hand with an analysis of the world that produced it.

Thus, in his autobiographical reflection, Rafael Sánchez leads his readers from the authoritarian and patriarchal world of his childhood and early youth, to the exuberant, disorganized, precarious, solidary, and generous world that he found on the streets of Caracas during the 1960s and 1970s, a world whose synthesis he later identifies in the cult of a maternal deity: María Lionza.

Some elements of Rafael Sánchez's experience provided him with a keen sensitivity that allowed him, later, to think and write a book that is arguably the best political anthropology of Venezuela that we have, and that is a referent in the comparative political anthropology of the Spanish American republics, namely *Dancing Jacobins*, a book that was published in 2016.[1] Perhaps most relevant among biographical elements was his father's illegitimacy, which undoubtedly helped Sánchez detect the hollowness that is characteristic of caudillo authority in Latin American countries and then to develop the thesis that Venezuela's political history is characterized by what he calls "monumental governmentality," wherein authority is not the emulsion of the kind of disciplinary institutions identified by Michel Foucault, but rather of the gigantism and monumentalization of the *caudillo*, who intimidates and seduces the free multitudes that crowd the public square with a hollow theatricality and with a more intimately administered impassioned violence. *Cara seria, culo rochelero*—a serious countenance with an impudent ass—this is the saying that, to Sánchez, summarizes the figure of the Father, of the *caudillo*, and of the State in Venezuela.

Rafael Sánchez's illegitimate father also expressed himself along those lines. In Havana, the man was at once an august tribune and a champion rumba dancer, who imposed his paternal authority by slapping down his oldest boy, terrifying him. Even so, Rafael's father did not quite manage to hide his own insufficiency: his social inferiority with regard to his wife, Rafael's mother, or his more diffuse social insecurity. In the end, cuffs and slaps were not enough for him to control his eldest son.

This biographical element—the illegitimacy of his father—helps Rafael Sánchez discover a social fact that, like Edgar Allan Poe's famous purloined letter, had lain hidden in plain sight. I have already said that this is the memoir of a remarkable anthropologist. Sánchez understood that the cultural history of the republic is a palimpsest where the cynical intimidation promoted from the State is dressed up in the sublimated person of the Liberator, but that this known fact develops in tandem with a no less important, exuberant development of a set of subject positions that Sánchez identifies with "The Mother," characterized by an openness to being possessed by an open-ended series of masks that ordinary people access in order to support one another and so to endure the challenges of a precarious social world that is always threatened by authority—threatened, for instance, by the police, who daily chased the young prostitutes that thronged the Plaza Altamira of Sánchez's youth. Those same young women provided our author with more solidarity, more tenderness, and more support than what he received in his paternal home.

"The night shall provide," said his friend Máximo, when Rafael was thinking about leaving his parents' house for good, without having anywhere else to go. Rafael does not linger too much on the difficulties that he faced as a result of having listened to Máximo, maybe because, as an anthropologist, he was more deeply impressed by something other than his own misfortunes. Sánchez is moved, instead, by the generosity that he encountered in the streets of downtown Caracas—the solidarity, the spontaneous show of affection, and the utopian promise that he experienced in fleeting encounters, sometimes even in the instant of an interlocking gaze.

Our author thus offers us an opening to the world that he discovered as a youth in the Plaza Altamira, in the Plaza Venezuela, in the hotels for prostitution where he lived and worked, as much as in the luxury hotels and restaurants where Rafael squatted and mooched in practices that his friend, Douglas, sublimated as claims for social justice. That is where Rafael Sánchez discovered the world and where he freed himself from the authoritarian charge of his childhood and early adolescence. Rafael banished himself from his parents' home and came to know love and friendship. And he surrendered himself also to books and to political militancy.

Except that he soon began to sniff out the verticality in militancy, the same monumentalized authoritarianism of "The Father." If it was not that, then what exactly was the "party line" that he had to repeat, meeting after meeting? So Sánchez eventually left his political militancy behind and decided to study anthropology. He then discovered the cult of María Lionza in a mountain in Venezuela, and with it a pedagogy, a mythology, and a ritual that managed to figure in both a symbolic and a practical dimension the practices that Venezuelans had joyously and painfully learned to apply though their long experience with dictatorship and with hollow oratory, and with everything that comes out of those monumentalized figures who always want to govern with a mixture of oratory and violence.

Rafael Sánchez's anthropological discovery—the dialectic between the authoritarianism of the Father, embodied in the monumentalized figure of the *caudillo*, and the solidarity of one thousand masks that sprouts up every day in the crowd—reminds me of every and any one of the great discoveries that anthropology has translated to the public: the discovery of the kula that surprised Malinowski, the Iroquois kinship that allowed for the creation of a broad political confederation, or more recently, the dialectic between positive and negative value that Nancy Munn discovered in her study of Gawa.[2]

Reconocimientos is, then, a singular text, a kind of Latin American cross between Montaigne and Malinowski, in which an anthropologist discovers in his own biography a key to understanding the collective history of a continent.

Notes

Introduction

1. Walter Benjamin, *Berlin Childhood around 1900*, trans. Howard Eiland (Cambridge, MA: Belknap Press of Harvard University Press, 2006 [1938]).

2. These aspects of Leiris's life, whose absence from *Manhood* Susan Sontag remarked in her foreword to the translated volume, are extensively documented in Leiris's memoir of Marcel Griaule's Dakar-Djibouti expedition, *Phantom Africa*. See Susan Sontag, "Foreword," in Michel Leiris, *Manhood: A Journey from Childhood into the Fierce Order of Virility*, trans. Richard Howard, intro Susan Sontag (Chicago: University of Chicago Press, 1984 [1939]), vii–xvii. See also Michel Leiris, *Phantom Africa*, trans. Brent Hayes Edwards (London: Seagull Books, 2017 [1934]).

3. Leiris, *Manhood*, 21.

4. In fact, the Venezuelan publisher ultimately changed the title to the more common, singular form of *Reconocimiento*. We nonetheless believe that the somewhat awkward and uncommon title more adequately reflects the many forms of recognition operative, sought, and refused in Sánchez's narrative.

5. While at the University of Chicago, Marshall Sahlins developed this concept to mediate between the two poles of Lévi-Strauss's thought, namely the historical and the structural, which Lévi-Strauss analogized to the vertical and the horizontal. Sahlins's arguments about the structure of conjuncture appear in two main works: *Historical Metaphors and Mythical Realities: Structure in the Early History of the Sandwich Islands Kingdom* (Ann Arbor: ASAO Special Publication, University of Michigan Press, 1981), and *Islands of History* (Chicago: University of Chicago Press, 1987). The concept was brought to bear on the question of the body and practice theory by Jean Comaroff in her book, *Body of Power, Spirit of Resistance* (Chicago: University of Chicago Press, 1985). Sánchez's thought in both *Dancing Jacobins* and *Reconocimientos* bears the impress of these mutually informing conversations, and was also influenced by Nancy Munn, whose later *The Fame of Gawa: A Symbolic Study of Value Transformation in a Massim Society* (Durham, NC: Duke University Press, 1992) took these questions in a more phenomenological direction. Sánchez nonetheless retained much of his earlier reading of Marxism—narrated in *Reconocimientos*—even as he embraced the ethical and political philosophy of Jacques Derrida, Philippe Lacoue-Labarthe, and Jean-Luc Nancy. His engagement with psychoanalysis also inflected his thinking in ways that were rarely embraced by disciplinary anthropology at Chicago.

6. Roland Barthes, *The Preparation of the Novel: Lecture Courses and Seminars at the Collège de France (1978–1979 and 1979–1980)*, trans. Kate Biggs, annotated by and intro. Nathalie Léger (New York: Columbia University Press, 2011), 8.

7. Barthes, *Preparation*, 8.

8. Barthes, *Preparation*, 9.

9. Barthes, *Preparation*, 11.

Reconocimientos: A Memoir of Becoming

1. In keeping with our decision to retain something of Rafael Sánchez's idiosyncratic English, as well as his recognition of the

symbolic coding and overdeterminations with which the sexed body is burdened, we have translated *"toda la región inferior de mi cuerpo"* as "all the inferior regions of my body." A more colloquial translation, emphasizing spatial and directional logics over symbolic values, might simply refer to these as lower regions.

2. Walter Benjamin, "The Storyteller: Observations on the Works of Nikolai Leskov," in *Selected Writings*, vol. 3: *1935–1938*, ed. Howard Eiland and Michael W. Jennings (Cambridge, MA: Harvard University Press, 2002), 142–66.

3. Jacques Lacan, *The Seminar of Jacques Lacan Book XVII, The Other Side of Psychoanalysis, 1969–1970*, ed. J. A. Miller, trans. R. Grigg (New York: Norton & Co, 2007), 112.

4. Claudio Lomnitz, *Nuestra América: My Family in the Vertigo of Translation* (New York; Other Press, 2021).

5. Adalber Salas Hernández, "Carta de Jamaica," in *Salvoconducto [Safe Conduct]* (Valencia: Editorial Pre-Textos/Ayuntamiento de Alcalá la Real, 2015), 82-84.

6. Jacques Derrida, *Passions* (Paris: Galilée, 1993), 64–65; Derrida, "Passions: An Oblique Offering," trans. David Wood, in *On the Name*, ed. Thomas Dutoit (Stanford, CA: Stanford University Press, 1995), 28.

7. Carlos E. Eire, *Waiting for Snow in Havana: Confessions of a Cuban Boy* (New York: Free Press, 2003).

8. It would be less literal and perhaps more colloquially familiar to translate this phrase, almost inassimilable to English, as a "space devoid of grace," but in this case, the figurative allusions seem more appropriate to the social scene, where a carnal devotion to saints and the illustration of angels is common.

9. Lorenzo García Vega, *Los Años des Orígines* (Madrid: Rialto Ediciones, 2018 [1978, by Monte Ávila Editores]).

10. Michael Taussig, *Magic of the State* (New York: Routledge, 1997).

11. Rafael Sánchez, *Dancing Jacobins: A Venezuelan Genealogy of Latin American Populism* (New York: Fordham University Press, 2016).

12. Jacques Derrida, "Plato's Pharmacy," in *Dissemination*,

trans. and intro. Barbara Johnson (Chicago: University of Chicago Press, 1981 [1972]), 63–171.

13. The reference is to Karl Marx, "The Eighteenth Brumaire of Louis Bonaparte," in *Surveys from Exile* (New York: Verso, 2010), 143–249.

14. Called a "Rosa de los vientos" in Spanish, the wind or compass rose is a figure of cartography in which all directions are figured on a compass.

15. Jean-Luc Nancy, *Being Singular Plural*, trans. Robert D. Richardson and Anne E. O'Byrne (Stanford, CA: Stanford University Press, 2000 [1996]).

16. Siegfried Kracauer, "The Mass Ornament," in *The Mass Ornament: Weimar Essays*, trans. Thomas Y. Levin (Cambridge, MA: Harvard University Press, 1995), 75–88.

17. I am thinking here of the North American civil rights movement; the so-called new social movements are something else, although I think that they do not completely avoid the characteristics of the first, but that is another topic.

18. Catherine Malabou, "The Crowd," *Oxford Literary Review* 27, no. 1 (2015): 25–44.

19. Malabou, "Crowd." As an aside, I would add here that, in my opinion, Malabou's critique is not fully justified; Canetti is not nearly as insensitive to reflexivity as she claims.

20. An *arepa* is a kind of food, and an *arepera* is the kiosk where they are purveyed.

21. Pierre Clastres, *Society against the State*, trans. Robert Hurley with Abe Stein (New York: Zone Books, 1980).

22. Philippe Lacoue-Labarthe and Jean-Luc Nancy, *Retreating the Political*, ed. Simon Sparks (New York: Routledge, 1997).

23. *Papillon* was originally released in 1973, directed by Franklin J. Schaffner, with a screenplay by Dalton Trumbo and Lorenzo Semple Jr.

24. A more colloquial translation of fuerza might be "strength," but it is such an elaborated concept in the María Lionza cult, and so imbricated with concepts of electrical

current as well as metaphysical eventfulness, that we have chosen to use the word "force."

25. Franz Kafka, "The Metamorphosis," in *The Complete Stories*, trans. Willa and Edwin Muir (New York: Schocken Books, 1977), 89–139.

26. Nancy, *Being Singular Plural*; Lacoue-Labarthe and Rancierè, *Retreating the Political*.

27. Rosalind C. Morris, "On the Subject of Spirit Mediumship in the Age of New Media," in *Trance Mediums and New Media*, ed. Heike Behrend, Anja Dreschke, and Martin Zillinger (New York: Fordham University Press, 2014), 25–55.

The Three Squares: Being, Having Been, Being Another

1. Rafael Sánchez, *Dancing Jacobins: A Venezuelan Genealogy of Latin American Populism* (New York: Fordham University Press, 2016).

2. Pierre Clastres's explorations of this conception of antipolitical society was developed on the basis of his work with the Guayaki Indians in Paraguay as well as the Yanomami in Venezuela, and appeared in *Chronicle of the Guayaki Indians*, trans. Paul Auster (New York: Zone, 1998 [1972]) as well as essays collected under the title *Society against the State*, trans. Robert Hurley and Abe Stein (New York: Zone, 1994 [1974]).

3. Jacques Derrida, *The Politics of Friendship*, trans. George Collins (New York: Verso, 2006 [1994]).

4. For an extended development of this hypothesis, see Luis Pérez-Oramas: *Venezuela Siglo XIX: arquitectura y estrategias simbólicas*, in *La cocina de Jurassic park y otros ensayos visuales* (Caracas: Fundación Polar, 1998), 225.

Afterword

1. Rafael Sánchez, *Dancing Jacobins: A Venezuelan Genealogy of Latin American Populism* (New York: Fordham University Press, 2016).

2. On the kula, see Bronislaw Malinowski, *Argonauts of the Western Pacific: An Account of Native Enterprise and Adventure in the Archipelagoes of Melanesian New Guinea* (New York: Dutton, 1922). Iroquois kinship was famously discussed in Lewis Henry Morgan's *Ancient Society* (New York: Henry Holt, 1877). Munn's work on positive and negative value appears in Nancy Munn, *The Fame of Gawa: A Symbolic Study of Value Transformation in a Massim Society* (Durham, NC: Duke University Press, 1992).

Rafael Sánchez (1950–2024) was senior lecturer at the Geneva Graduate Institute. He is the author of *Dancing Jacobins: A Venezuelan Genealogy of Latin American Populism* (2016).

Rosalind C. Morris is Professor of Anthropology at Columbia University. Her most recent books are *Unstable Ground: The Lives, Deaths, and Afterlives of Gold in South Africa* (2025) and, with William Kentridge, *Accounts and Drawings from Underground* (2021). Her most recent film is the documentary *We Are Zama Zama* (2021).

Igor Barreto is a Venezuelan poet, editor, and translator. He has been Director of Publications at the Museo Jacobo Borges in Caracas, Director of the Cinemateca Nacional, Director of Collections of the Fundación de Etnomusicología y Folklore, and Director of Imprenta Anauco.

Luis Pérez-Oramas is a Venezuelan poet, art historian, and curator. He is the author of eleven volumes of poetry and numerous catalogue texts and critical essays. In 2011, he was Curatorial Director of the Bienal de São Paulo. From 2006 to 2017, he was Latin American Art Curator at the Museum of Modern Art in New York City.

Claudio Lomnitz is Campbell Family Professor of Anthropology at Columbia University. He is the author, most recently, of *Sovereignty and Extortion: A New State Form in Mexico* (Durham: Duke University Press, 2024).

www.ingramcontent.com/pod-product-compliance
Lightning Source LLC
Chambersburg PA
CBHW031156020426
42333CB00013B/689